"Mystery Babylon"

"Mystery Babylon"
The Coming Microchip Economy

Henry W. Vandergriff

Lamb Publishing

Printed in the USA by Sheridan Books, Inc. for,
Lamb Publishing, 4519 Laurel Hills Road, Raleigh NC 27612

All scripture quotations, unless otherwise indicated, are taken from the New King James Version. Copyright © 1982 by Thomas Nelson, Inc. Used by permission. All rights reserved.

Cover Design by Senior Graphics Designer and Artist, Lant Elrod

Photography by Commercial Photographer, Robert A. Flynn

Prayer Partners: Anthony Godley, Edith Jackson, Don Rayno, Peter Harrison and Van Vandergriff

Administrative Counselors: Lisa Harrod, Donna Blanchard

Editing Consultants: Donna Blanchard, Tim Harrod, Edith Jackson and Chief Editor Rob Flynn

Written: Fall of 1998   First Printing: 1999   Second Printing 2000

See Web Page: MysteryBabylon.net

ISBN 0-615-11839-9

Library of Congress Card Number (LCCN) 00-105009

Chapter	Contents	Page

Preface

In order to facilitate the reader concerning "Mystery Babylon," it is appropriate to explain the author's understanding of Christian salvation. The governing principles of personal salvation are the same principles that will give its adherents victory over any obstacle of the future. I will put forth these principles as briefly as possible and with much simplicity. Let me acknowledge the source of my understanding is from reading the Bible and from Godly men who have shared their love for God and the scriptures with me through preaching, personal fellowship and church attendance. Moreover, God has inspired with the presence of the Holy Spirit in moments of prayer and meditation.

As I read the creation account of Genesis, it is apparent to me that Adam and Eve fell from the grace of God through disobedience and since then all of mankind has inherited a spirit of rebellion against God. The Bible is a written history of God's love for man and desire for personal fellowship with man. God's love for creation compelled Him to send Jesus Christ to the cross to bear our sins. This opportunity for salvation is expressed clearly in John 3:16, "For God so loved the world that He gave His only begotten Son, that whoever believes in Him should not perish but have everlasting life."

The actual point of salvation and its governing principles of our relationship to God can be found in Romans 10:9-10+13, "that if you confess with your mouth the Lord Jesus and believe in your heart that God has raised Him from the dead, you will be saved. For with the heart one believes unto to righteousness, and with the mouth confession is made unto salvation... For whoever calls on the name of the Lord shall be saved." Within this passage are four identifiable conditions for salvation.

First, we must believe the message. That God loves us so much that He sent Jesus to pay the penalty of our sins by dying on the cross. We must believe that God desires to fellowship with us and has our best interest at heart. History records the event of Jesus' life and death two thousand years ago and our calendars remind us each year of our lives, "A.D., Anno Domini" in the year of our Lord. However, do we believe the message? Believing is the first step to bringing us into a right standing with God.

Second, we must embrace Jesus as Lord. Lordship means to allow Him to be the boss. If you get a job cleaning a restaurant and the boss asks you to mop the floor, what are you communicating if you answer, "no, I don't do mops?" If management relents and instructs you to clean the windows, how will they respond if you say, "perhaps later?" If your superior demands that you wipe down the tables and you declare, "I need a coffee break," chances are the employer will realize that you did not really want a job, but a paycheck. He will soon realize that he was never really your boss and therefore you are no longer his employee. Making Jesus Lord means to allow Him to be the boss in our lives. Jesus said, "If you love Me, keep My commandments" (John 14:15).

Thirdly, we must confess with our mouth, Jesus as Lord. Confession is an intricate part of our salvation relationship. Because of marriage vows, I wear a wedding band. When I am with my wife, she does not want me to walk ten feet in front of her or ten feet behind her. She wants me to hold her hand. When we are with a crowd of people, especially women, she finds it comforting to know that her man is acknowledging her preeminence by holding her close. Those actions and the ring are a reminder that I not only said yes to her forever, but also confirmed no to all others in the intimate relationship we enjoy. The Apostle Paul wrote, "for I am not ashamed of the gospel of Christ, for it is the power of God to salvation for everyone who believes...." (Romans 1:16). The power of confession brings the believer's name before the grace and favor of God Almighty. Jesus declared, "whoever confesses Me before men, him I will also confess before My Father who is in heaven" (Matthew 10:32).

Lastly, we must call upon His name. If a young man is interested in a young maiden, he must pick up the telephone and call if he is ever going to meet her at the coffee shop. So often, doubt and fear overcomes the suitor and all is lost because of this paralyses. Of course, he is in awe of her beauty, enamoured by her character and even aware of her interest to reciprocate the relationship, but doubt and fear ruins every relationship. Jesus implores us, "Ask, and it will be given to you; seek, and you will find; knock, and it will be opened to you" (Matthew 7:7). As we trust Jesus and call upon His name, a great adventure awaits us, as we explore all that God has for us when He chose to create us.

Many challenges lay ahead as social architects pursue mankind's utopian dream to form a world government, Biblically called "Mystery Babylon." Jesus said, "For then there will be great tribulation, such as has not been since the beginning of the world until this time, no, nor ever shall be" (Matthew 24:21). During that time, Christians will discover the governing principles of salvation will be the same principles that will deliver them in every tribulation. No circumstance or hardship can possibly be greater than the need for personal salvation. Just as God has redeemed us to a personal relationship with Him, He will lead us to victory in "Mystery Babylon."

In the generation to come, victory will be ours as we believe God loves us and has our best interest at heart. Secondly, He will lead and guide us as we allow Him to be Lord or the boss who directs our lives. Thirdly, our confession of Jesus will set us apart from the world and put a distinction between Christians and the loyal subjects of "Mystery Babylon." Lastly, as we call upon the Lord, we will be delivered or saved from the enemies of God. These four governing principles will cause Christians to triumph over Satan's fury and bring God glory through our obedience. May God inspire you in the reading of these pages and strengthen your faith.

<>< Henry Vandergriff, Author

"And when they had preached the gospel to that city and made many disciples, they returned…strengthening the souls of the disciples, exhorting them to continue in the faith, and saying, 'We must through many tribulations enter the kingdom of God.'"

Paul and Barnabus
(Acts 14:21-22)

Chapter 1

Jesus Speaks in Babylon
"The Latter Days"

*"Then Daniel...made the decision known...that they might
seek mercies from the God of heaven concerning this
secret, so that Daniel and his companions might not
perish with the rest of the wise men of Babylon."*
Daniel 2:17-18

God has given us many hints through prophecy to
forewarn of the Anti-Christ's kingdom called Mystery
Babylon and to encourage us to wait for the true kingdom
and Revelation of Jesus Christ. Jesus told Daniel in
Babylon, "I have come to make you understand what
shall befall your people in the latter days...I will show
you that which is noted in the scripture of truth" (Daniel
10:6+14+20-21 compare with Revelation 1:12-16). Jesus
said what would happen to Daniel's people in the latter
days, could be understood from the scriptures that were
already written at that time, during Israel's captivity in
Babylon. If we take our Lord's words literally, then one
could simply study the Old Testament types or shadows,
and the OT scriptures would reveal what would happen to
God's people in the latter days. Fortunately, we have the
added witness of the New Testament as well.

Just as Jesus spoke to Daniel, He also said to the
Apostle John, "The Revelation of Jesus Christ, which
God gave Him to show His servants-things, which must
shortly take place" (Revelation 1:1). The Book of
Revelation is the picture of Jesus our savior being
revealed or in other words the revelation of Jesus Christ!
It begins with Jesus exhorting His church to a deeper,

purer walk with God. He then tells of the Anti-Christ who takes dominion over the whole world, his kingdom is known as Mystery Babylon. Through this kingdom the Anti-Christ, also known as the beast persecutes the saints, even to death for refusing to worship his image. This does not please God, who then brings forth the judgment of Mystery Babylon and reveals Jesus Christ to punish the world and to set up His own kingdom.

When you compare the Old Testament writings about ancient Babylon, with the New Testament writings about Mystery Babylon, you find an interesting parallel. The Old Testament prophets, Isaiah, Jeremiah, and Ezekial exhorted the people of God to a deeper, purer walk with God. They foretell of a vicious tyrant named Nebuchadnezzar, also given the nature of a beast, who is king over the Babylonian Empire and his advancing kingdom is taking dominion over the world. Like the Anti-Christ of Revelation, Nebuchaddnezzar also persecutes the saints with death for refusing to worship his image. Likewise, this does not please God who judges Babylon and its king, revealing one like unto the "Son of Man," in the fiery furnace.

God in His loving kindness reveals the future, so we will understand what He is doing and not be deceived. Consider this truth, "I am the Lord that is my name: and my glory I will not give to another, nor My praise to graven images. Behold, the former things have come to pass, and new things do I declare: before they spring forth I tell you of them" (Isaiah 42:8-9). In other words, the scriptures reveal enough of the Anti-Christ in both the Old and New Testaments, that we should not be surprised by his appearance, and certainly not willing to worship the image of the beast. For we know the true God who forewarns us, so we might pursue a deeper, purer walk with God, waiting for the true kingdom and our savior Jesus Christ!

My Personal Journey

In 1971, as a young teen, I made a decision to follow Jesus Christ as Lord. This change of heart brought a new spirit of dialogue between my grandfather and I. He had been a Christian for many years, and the fondest memory of him was the joy of the Lord he displayed, when he would come down the steps from prayer. He would be aglow with the presence of the Lord.

As a babe in Christ, I recall sharing with him the excitement I felt about the hope of the rapture (I still do). His heart was always rejoicing with mine in the expectation we have of the rapture. However, grandfather would always caution by quoting this scripture,

"Let no one deceive you by any means; for that Day will not come unless the falling away comes first, and the man of sin is revealed, the son of opposition"
(2 Thessalonians 2:3).

My pondering of this scripture and the passion by which he would share it with me, was always in conflict with what I was being taught in church. The popular notion is a Pre-Tribulation Rapture. And yet, in my heart I could always hear the echoing of this passage, as Christians we will witness the coronation of the Anti-Christ. But when will these things be?

The next piece of my personal puzzle concerning future events came during a college marketing class. The study began to focus on point of purchase machines and how the business world was going to handle the burgeoning lines of customers at the check out counter. The professor began to share with us the new technology that IBM had been developing since the 1950's. It was called the UPC symbol (Universal Product Code), also known as the bar code.   As we began studying this simple series of black bars, which is now on all products and represents all the pertinent product information necessary for buying and selling, the Holy Spirit began to speak to me.

His friendly voice reminded me of the Revelation of John on the isle of Patmos. Revelation 1:1 says this, "The Revelation of Jesus Christ, which God gave Him to show His servants-things which must shortly take place." As we proceed through the chapters, we find a prediction about the Anti-Christ.

"He causes all, both small and great, rich and poor, free and slave, to receive a mark on their right hand or their foreheads, and that **no one may buy or sell except one who has the mark** or the name of the beast, or the number of his name" (Revelation 13:16-17).

Now I did not understand it all, but I did know the Holy Spirit was reminding me of what Jesus had shown His servants. The day would come when they would experience a time in which the world would no longer buy and sell with money, but instead with some sort of mark. From that day forward, I have been intrigued with the successful growth of the UPC technology. Today, virtually every point of purchase machine utilizes the sophisticated laser reading of bar codes on every imaginable product, including mail. One thing is for certain, we are buying and selling, and *a mark is part of every transaction!*

But the scriptures tell us that a mark will be on our right hand or forehead, isn't it a leap to suggest this mark will be tattooed to our physical bodies? After all, what cosmopolitan woman in her right mind would allow a small half-inch UPC symbol to mar her beauty? Perhaps the answer is as close as our pets. Our local animal society offers a service; a small microchip can be implanted into the mane of our pets! If the pet is ever lost, anyone can take the pet to a local shelter and have it scanned. The chip records all the important information regarding the animal, thus alerting the anxious owner to its whereabouts. The thought occurred to me, if they can do that to pets, how much longer will it be until they are suggesting the insertion of the microchip into the right hand or forehead of humans? Apparently the time is near.

The Inventor of the Bar Code

Have you ever heard of Joseph Woodlake? Some years ago President Bush made a verbal gaffe in marveling over the UPC technology. The late 1980's President was on a public relations outing when he commented on the wonderful new technology at the check out counter of a local store. The gaffe was the technology wasn't new, it had been around for over a decade. His gaffe revealed the cavalier lifestyle of a politician so catered by White House servants; he didn't even know what common folks experience everyday. In an effort to quench the onslaught of negative media, the President invited the inventor of the technology, Joseph Woodlake to the White House in a ceremony to honor him.

The evening newscast revealed that Mr. Woodlake lived in my hometown. I proceeded to call him to inquire about the ins and outs of this system for buying and selling. He is a wonderful man, and very informative. He shared with me that IBM had asked him in the 1950's to begin work on this project, of discovering a way to expedite the process of buying, selling, and reordering, all in one exchange to enhance the value of IBM's point of purchase machines. He explained to me, the laser reads the light and darkness of the bar codes. One part acknowledges the product and deducts it from inventory, and the other part proclaims the price and tallies the product for future reorder. He said the numbers under the black bars mean absolutely nothing to the laser. They were there only for human comprehension.

Universal Personal Identification Code

He then began to explain other areas of research that will impact our future. Just as the UPC symbol is designed to catalogue every product on the face of the earth, other systems are being designed to identify every person on the planet, called the universal personal identification code (UPIC). Several areas being researched were mentioned. First is the laser scanning of the thumbprint. Second is the voiceprint of the vocal chords; third is the laser scanning of the eye's iris. And lastly is the use of the bar code on microchips.

It was explained to me that the microchip has the ability to receive all the information that is presently on the magnetic strip of your credit cards, along with any other personal history that would be appropriate. Whala! It doesn't take a revelation, crystal ball, or prophet to figure out which of these technologies will eventually become the predominate mode of use. All of them will be used in various degrees, and for numerous applications. However, since the machinery is already in place throughout the business world, it will be cost effective to simply continue using them with the added application of reading your microchip instead of your credit-debit card.

How? By simply implanting it through a needle under the skin of your hand or forehead, just like our pets. The laser scanners of the world will read the microchip deducting financial transactions and tracking all buying and selling. It is so small that its appearance will be that of a tiny mark, less than a birthmark and possibly unseen. Cosmopolitan women will accept it and consumers will receive it because of it's minor physical inconvenience, and enormous financial accessibility.

Present Technology Implants

At the mere suggestion of this idea, people often scowl as if this is ridiculous. But who would have dreamed fifty years ago that man could actually transplant a human heart? Today it is mere routine, and a couple of days in the hospital. Today people walk around with many implants of man's making. People with metal screws and plates in their skeleton frequently set off the metal detectors at the airport. People with pacemakers are warned with signs in the local convenience store about public microwave ovens. Women have implants of collagen for wrinkles and silicone for breasts. Teenage girls' line up at the public health clinic to get a birth control device called Norplant injected into their arms. And the optical industry has now pioneered the implanting of microchips into the eye's retina to enhance seeing. Microchips are presently being designed so small, that in the future they will actually flow through the blood stream and monitor the recipient's health. With technology's ever increasing advancements, why should we be surprised to hear of man's pursuit to identify every person on the planet with a microchip that will appear as a small mark?

Present Monetary Problems

America will lead the way with this microchip economy. The masses are already being told that solutions must be sought for several problems with our present monetary system.

Identity fraud is on the increase as clever thieves learn how to rip off your identity and exhaust your good credit. These modern robbers mar your credit history, while grossly inconveniencing you as you try to sort out the credit woes with your lending officers.

Thieves are picking up your identity in simple ways. They monitor internet transactions and listen to cell phones as you give your credit card number for a purchase. Now with the availability of personal magnetic scanners, the waiter at the local restaurant can steal your identity in the short time frame of taking your card to ring up your meal and returning the receipt to be signed. Within twenty-four hours, your identity could be sold and your credit exhausted by identity purchasers around the world.

Counterfeiting has become so precise with store bought scanners and laser printers, that crooks are creating small bills that are fooling the scrutiny of the most astute businessmen. In addition, white-collar thieves are scanning and printing payroll checks of community businesses and cashing them at local banks.

The extortion chaos is causing alarm for our community leaders, as people scream for answers. Eventually the solution will be proposed to accept the universal personal identification code and move to a microchip economy.

The Time Paradox

How close are we to this system?   Recently during a luncheon with several Pastors, I shared my heart about these future events. One of the Pastors shared his conversation with a parishioner of his, who sat on the board of a local hospital. The subject of implanting newborn babies in the obstetrics department was discussed. He told us the idea was turned down, because we lived in the Bible belt of the south and it would be met with opposition.   However, consumer resistance will eventually be worn away and this system will be embraced.

The Prophet Daniel was told, "Shut up the words, and seal the book, even to the time of the end: many shall run to and fro, and knowledge shall be increased" (Daniel 12:4). The words are sealed, but not forever, just until the time when knowledge shall increase and men shall run to and fro.   When Orville and Wilbur Wright made it known they were developing a flying machine, a New York City newspaper said, "travel by air is still a thousand years in the future!"   Since that time, we have seen the amazing development of the airline industry. A hundred years ago, we were still in the horse and buggy days. Less than fifty years earlier it took six months to go from Independence, Missouri, via the Oregon Trail to California. Now you can be there in an afternoon on a non-stop flight from New York to Los Angeles. Boeing Corporation recently announced the development of the personal family flying machine and unveiled a functional prototype.   They expect to make available a personal aircraft for your family that is affordable in the coming decades. It is supposed to revolutionize the way we live, alleviating overcrowding in the cities by allowing people to fly to work or the marketplace.   One has to admit, knowledge has increased, and men run to and fro. We live in the information age and knowledge is increasing at warp speed.   Now is the season for the words to be unsealed!

Technology has built a world marketplace via the Internet. You can buy and sell through your personal computer instantly across the world, and have overnight delivery. Soon cash will be likened to vinyl records, as society embraces the prophetic time of buying and selling with a mark on your right hand. The convergence of prophecy and technology has brought us to a pivotal apex, when Christ's return is imminent.

Each day the Lord delays His coming draws us closer to the moment the cash-less system will be introduced. Along with that moment is the revealing of Satan himself, manifesting his hatred towards God and His followers. His persecution will have Christians executed for their refusal to worship his image. We must adequately prepare our hearts for this season of violence. We must carefully consider the words of the Apostle Paul, "Let no one deceive you by any means; for that Day will not come unless the falling away comes first, and the man of sin is revealed, the son of opposition" (2 Thessalonians 2:3).

The Wide Gate

The universal personal identification code is the embryo of the cash-less system that will eventually be seized and manipulated by the future Anti-Christ, for the purpose of controlling and governing the nations. But much more is at stake than the simple ego and political ambitions of an individual, or the profit of a greedy business corporation. Satan himself as the beast will capitalize upon this season of market economy, for the defining purpose of drawing a myriad into a utopian government design to exalt man. However, its result is the wide gate of destruction leading to hell, for all who take the mark will lose their opportunity for salvation according to this scripture.

"If anyone worships the beast and his image, and receives his mark…he shall be tormented with fire and brimstone…and the smoke of their torment ascends forever and ever; and they have no rest day or night who worship the beast and his image, and whoever receives the mark…." (Revelation 14:9-11).

We are on the threshold of this new economic system. My burden is for the body of Christ, who has been indoctrinated with the idea that we are going to be snatched out prior to the appearance of the Anti-Christ. There seems to be, a who cares mentality. The average Christian still does not witness with any urgency and seems to be caught up in worldliness to the point of slumbering. Their thinking seem to be, no one is going to suffer, or endure any hardship; after all, we'll be gone. I hope they are right about this Pre-Anti-Christ Rapture. I would love nothing more than to go on home with my savior. But deep down I know this generation has a calling for the end time purpose of our Father. We will not be "deceived by any means." Instead, we have been singled out and ordained for this dispensation, to prepare the world for the triumphal return of our Lord, and His

victory over "the man of sin, the son of opposition." In
the last days, Jesus said there would be:

> "**The hour of trial** which shall come upon the whole
> world, to test those who dwell on the earth"
> (Revelation 3:10).

This test is centered on the mark of the Anti-Christ.
Men will fail the spiritual test if they receive the mark,
but pass if they have the spiritual fortitude to live by faith
and refuse the coming microchip's implantation,
choosing to trust Christ as their source of sustenance.

If the Lord should tarry, the Anti-Christ will rise to
power and require all people to take the mark, and those
who don't will be punished with death. Christians who
thought they would be raptured out will be disillusioned,
grasping for answers in the face of being shut out of the
job market, unable to buy groceries and the basic
elements of living for refusing to take the mark.
Unfortunately, many will be caught unprepared, lacking
understanding and they will succumb to the great falling
away.

God Wrote the End

However, God foretells these future events and will
demonstrate to the world the faithfulness of His saints, a
people "without spot or blemish," citizens of the true
kingdom. The church will exemplify its finest hour. The
witness of their patience, faith and sacrificial living
towards God, by refusing the mark, will usher in the
greatest harvest of souls to the kingdom ever known in
the history of man. God will vindicate His church by
pouring out His wrath, punishing all that have taken the

mark. At last, Christ will return to gather His bride, to destroy the Anti-Christ and set up His kingdom to be ruled by His faithful saints.

It is my intent as a watchman, to sound the trumpet regarding the coming social upheaval, the rise of Mystery Babylon. As the Lord tarries, we must prepare our hearts to endure the trials that are coming to this generation. The destiny of our souls depends upon our willingness to obey. Jesus said, "He who endures to the end shall be saved" (Matthew 24:13). The Apostle Paul encourages us, "But you, brethren, are not in darkness, so that this Day should over take you as a thief" (1Thessalonians 5:4). The warnings are there, provided for us by a loving God who desires that we are "more than conquerors" in this day and hour. The victory is ours! It will be the solid commitment of Christians who spread the triumphant word that will prepare the world for the greatest revival ever known. Let's begin by discovering the Babylon of old and its implications for today. For Mystery Babylon is on the rise!

Chapter Two

Revelation's Mystery Babylon
"The New Revealed is the Old Concealed"

"There is a God in heaven who reveals secrets, and He has made known to the King Nebuchaddnezzar what will be in the latter days." Daniel 2:28

A good mystery has several components. There are diverse characters involved in a plot, along with several subplots. Each personality has a motive connecting them to the possibility of the crime. The suspense is tantalized by each additional bit of information, until the mystery is crystallized with the surprise ending of who done it!

The stories of Biblical Babylon are recorded for our discernment. Each one is a clue to the surprise ending of Revelation's Mystery Babylon. Speaking of these passages, the Apostle Paul reflects, "These things happened...as examples, and they were written for our admonition, on whom the ends of the ages have come" (1Corinthians10:11). Through these examples, we can assemble Mystery Babylon. Rev. Jerry Falwell once said, "The new morality is nothing more than the old immorality." It is the same with Revelation's Mystery Babylon.

Nimrod's Babylon

In Genesis 11:1-10 we find the ancient story of Nimrod (Gensis10:10) who led the people of the world in building a city and tower. According to Babylonian tradition, the god Marduk founded the city. The top of the tower was crowned with a temple, where the god was thought to descend for intercourse with mankind. They not only had a single language, but they were of a single heart in their purpose for living. When the Lord came down to see the tower, He was impressed! So much that God marveled, "now nothing will be restrained from them, which they have imagined to do."

God decided to end it for one simple reason. *It was rebellion!* The people committed themselves, one *to another,* not to God. They said, "Let *us* build *us* a city and a tower, whose top may reach to the heavens," not let us build unto God for His glory! They declared, "Let *us* make *us* a name," instead of exalting God's name. They vowed, "Lest we be scattered abroad upon the face of the whole earth," in direct opposition to God's earlier command on the sixth day of creation, "Be fruitful, and multiply, and replenish the earth, and subdue it" (Genesis 1:28).

The lesson learned is that a rebellious spirit seeks to dwell in self-exaltation, not in honor of the Lord. Therefore God scattered them and called the place Babel. It means confusion or mixture. Whenever we live for self, exalting our name and our purposes, rest assured that we will find ourselves in a state of confusion, lacking understanding. Isn't this exactly what happens to people who do not know the Lord? Their desire to live for self blinds them and they haven't the slightest comprehension of the gospel. Why? Confusion means: the state of bewilderment. They don't know they are blind, in fact, they think they are right. The scriptures speak this truth about people who are deceived, "If our gospel is veiled, it is veiled to those who are perishing, whose minds the god of this age has blinded, who do not believe, lest the light of the gospel of the glory of Christ, who is the image of God, should shine on them" (1 Corinthians 4:3-4).

No wonder Mystery Babylon of Revelation is referred to as a harlot (Revelation 17:1-2). Harlots give themselves to many lovers without discretion. God is revealing this worldliness of mixing one's self with pride and self-exaltation is the spirit of Mystery Babylon! This spirit is going to pervade mankind, to the point of giving themselves to the Anti-Christ with one heart and purpose. The only exception will be the wise behavior of those whose names are written in the Lamb's Book of Life.

Nebuchadnezzar's Babylon

During his lifetime, Nebuchadnezzar established an empire, whose dominion covered the known world of his time. He defeated the nation of Israel and took the people away captive. A young Israelite name Daniel was trained to be one of his advisers, and was called upon to interpret a dream for the king. Nebuchadnezzar's dream is significant to us, because it is a picture of "What shall be in the latter days" (Daniel 2:28). We will examine this in greater detail later.

Like Nimrod, Nebuchadnezzar demonstrated the same spirit of pride and arrogance towards God. He was repeatedly told his Babylonian kingdom had been established by God (Daniel 2:21, 37, 47 and 3:17, 25, 32). Despite God's revelations to his heart, the king declared, "Is not this great Babylon that **I have built** for the house of the kingdom by **the might of my power**, and for the honor of **my majesty**?" (Daniel 4:30). For this reason, the name Babylon has become synonymous with the spirit of pride, arrogance and self-exaltation. Patiently, God gave Nebuchadnezzar a year to repent of his attitude, and when he refused, God judged him by giving him the heart of a beast for seven years. The Anti-Christ of

Mystery Babylon is likewise referred to as a beast!

After seven years, his understanding returned because he lifted his eyes up to heaven. He lived out his years worshipping and acknowledging God in his life. His last recorded words were, "Those who walk in pride, he is able to abase" (Daniel 4:37). Nebuchadnezzar's life was ordained by God to be a historical picture of the Anti-Christ and Mystery Babylon. He finished his life honoring God, but God used his carnal seasons to paint a canvas of the future for all to see. More about this later, suffice it now to say Babylon continues to reveal the pride of man.

Belshazzar's Babylon

Daniel chapter five shares the story of Babylon under Nebuchadnezzar's descendant, Belshazzar. As the new king, he continues to flourish the Babylonian kingdom until one day he makes a great feast. His celebrations include using the vessels taken from the house of God in Jerusalem for toasting the gods of gold, silver and materialism. It is at this moment that Belshazzar sees a man's hand, writing on the wall. The phrase is unintelligible and he summons Daniel for an interpretation. Daniel reminds Belshazzar of his father's history of waxing prideful, and that it was God who had given the kingdom to his father and sentenced him to seven years grazing grass for his arrogance. Daniel admonishes Belshazzar, "You...have not humbled your heart, although you knew all this...and lifted up yourself against the Lord of heaven...and praised the gods of silver and gold...and the God who holds your breath in His hand...you have not glorified" (Daniel 5:22-23).

The natural progression of the Babylonian mentality

believes that somehow one has gained power and wealth, and done so without the help of God. Moses forewarned the children of Israel, after he had led them out of Egypt and brought them into the Promised Land by saying, "When you have eaten and are satisfied, praise the Lord your God for the good land he has given you. Be careful that you do not forget the Lord your God ...and say to yourself, my power and the strength of my hands have produced this wealth for me. But remember the Lord your God, for it is he who gives you the ability to produce wealth, and so confirms the covenant" (Deuteronomy 8:10-18 NIV). Hence, the evolving Babylonian spirit adds a new dimension to its pride, the idea that money and wealth are *ours*, not God's.

"MENE, MENE, TEKEL, UPHARSIN," the handwriting seen on the wall by Belshazzar was interpreted to mean this, "God has numbered your kingdom and it is finished, you are weighed in the balances and found lacking, and your kingdom is given to another." You can be sure Mystery Babylon of Revelation will be like Belshazzar's Babylon. When men begin to praise buying, selling, wealth and materialism to the point of worshipping a clever politician (Anti-Christ) who has devised a world economy by which all may participate and prosper, the "handwriting will be on the wall." For shortly thereafter, the angel cries, "Babylon the great is fallen" (Revelation 18:2). Their kingdom will be found lacking and given to another, Jesus Christ!

Babylon the Tourist Attraction

Isaiah the prophet foretold the destruction of Babylon by the Medes, a people who could care less about their gold and silver. "Babylon, the glory of the kingdoms, the beauty of the Chaldees' Excellency, shall be as when God overthrew Sodom and Gomorrah. **It shall never be inhabited, neither shall it be dwelt in from generation to generation**... but wild beasts of the desert shall lie there...." (Isaiah 13:19-21). The city of Babylon and its influence as an empire continued to lose its significance in the succeeding generations. Though many invading conquerors sought to rebuild and restore her former glory, it was all to no avail, God had spoken.

Jeremiah echoed the sentiments of Isaiah, "A sound of battle is in the land, and of great destruction...Babylon is become a desolation among the nations" (Jeremiah 50:22-23). He even told us the reason for God's eternal judgment, "For she has been proud against the Lord, against the Holy One of Israel." (v.29) Why am I not surprised? Today, a short drive from Baghdad, Iraq, the remnants of archeological Babylon exist only in the resurrection of a few buildings for tourism purposes. There, tourists can return and remember her former glory. During the Gulf War the United States military drove within fifty miles of Babylon. Our TV screens were filled with images of desert wilderness. In the surrounding plains of the vast horizon, a few wild camels could be seen from time to time.

Babylon Lives in Spirit!

Jeremiah's proclamations tell us several important characteristics about the Babylonian spirit. He says, "Set up the standards upon the walls of Babylon, make the watch strong, ...the inhabitants of Babylon ...that dwell upon many waters, abundant in treasures, your end is come, and the measure of thy covetousness" (Jeremiah 51:12-13).

First, he acknowledges the Babylonian spirit dwells on many waters. "Many waters" is a Biblical phrase referring to a worldwide acceptance of an ideology (Revelation 17:15). Thus, this spirit of pride, arrogance, money and materialism has permeated all of society. Secondly, he is saying God has set standards on the perimeter of Babylon. This spirit, like a dog on a leash, will only be allowed a designated space, until God's judgment: "Your end is come." The entire chapter of Revelation eighteen describes Mystery Babylon's judgment and the mourning of the multitudes at the collapse of the commercial system. The judgement is the final boundary or measure of her covetousness.

Jeremiah continues his prophetic admonishments. "Flee out of the midst of Babylon, and deliver every man his soul: be not cut off in her iniquity; for this is the time of the Lord's vengeance; ...Babylon has been a golden cup in the Lord's hand, that made all the earth drunken: the nations have drunken of her wine; therefore the nations are mad. Babylon is suddenly fallen and destroyed...." (Jeremiah 51:6-8). In a twist of irony, God says it was Babylon in His hand being used for God's purposes. That purpose was to teach God's people about His plans and forewarn them of the judgment to come.

Note the impact of the prophecy. Mystery Babylon the spirit falls suddenly, much like Belshazzar's reign in the height of his glory! Revelation 18:2+10 declares, "Babylon the great is fallen... Alas, alas that great city Babylon, that mighty city! For in one hour is thy judgment is come."

The Babylonian spirit makes the nations drunk. Drunkenness causes one to lose his reasoning faculties. The spirit even drives them mad, or to the point of craziness! Certainly no one would take the mark of the beast in Mystery Babylon if they thought it would cause them to lose their salvation (Revelation 14:9-11). This is precisely the point. Their desire to buy, sell and have materialism at the expense of worshipping the Anti-Christ overrides their good conscious towards God.

God instructed Abraham, "Get out of your country, [Ur of the Chaldees was Babylon]... and I will bless you" (Genesis 12:1-2). Jeremiah says, "Flee out of the midst of Babylon and deliver every man his soul." The Apostle John says of Mystery Babylon, "Come out of her, my people, lest you share in her sins and lest you receive of her plagues. For her sins have reached unto heaven, and God has remembered her iniquities" (Revelation 18:4-5). Jesus echoed this same truth, "For what shall it profit a man if he gains the whole world, and loses his own soul?" (Mark 8:36).

Today's Mystery Babylon

Often in conversations, I have heard people refer to Babylon as New York City because it is home to the United Nations. Others have insisted Rome, because it is the home of the Catholic Church. However, these are guesses in "the who done it" of Mystery Babylon. Each identity certainly plays a contributing role, but as we discovered from the Old Testament characters, *Babylon no longer exists as a geographical location!* Instead, *Mystery Babylon is a spirit that survives as the culmination of man's pride and self-exaltation. It is the spirit of self-preservation, pursuing private wealth and materialism, to the exclusion of God.*

This spirit certainly mingles itself with the politician's pork barrel as well as the religious Elmer Gantry. *Babel means confusion and mixture.* In the next chapter, we will see how this mixture of man's heart has many subplots on many different levels of human life, from the individual dealing with the temptation of covetousness, to the yearning of third world nations for western goods. As the Lord tarries, each covetous stream will culminate into the river of our main plot, the rise of Mystery Babylon.

Chapter 3

Mystery Babylon is Alive and Well!
"The Covetous Spirit"

"In the last days perilous times will come: for men will be...lovers of themselves, lovers of money...lovers of pleasure rather than lovers of God...." 2 Timothy 3:1-3

The ambulance came to an abrupt halt, as the paramedic leaped out in disbelief! There before him in the icy snow was the torn wreckage of a brand new Lexus. Expecting the worst, he scarcely imagined anyone could have survived the impact. Suddenly, he heard a moan and rushed to the man's side exclaiming, "I can't believe it!"

"What?" said the mangled semi conscious man.

"Your car is demolished, but you're alive," quipped the paramedic!

"Oh no, my Lexus, my beautiful Lexus," groaned the injured yuppie.

"But you're breathing," exclaimed the Good Samaritan!

"My ski trip is ruined," lamented the young executive.

"But you're alive, you've lost an arm, but you're still alive!" marveled the arriving police officer! Silence gripped the night as the driver grasped the weight of the moment. Gasping, he cried, "my Rolex, where's my Rolex!"

This story is hysterical, but it is a sad commentary on the twenty-first century. History records a cyclical carnal truth; men value the pride of wealth, more than life. Jesus told a similar story to illustrate this kingdom principle: "beware of covetousness, for one's life does not consist in the things he possesses." His parable was about a rich farmer who prospered in everything he planted. His harvest was so great he tore down his barns and built bigger barns. After successfully completing the project, he reflected, "Soul, you have many goods laid up for many years; take your ease; eat, drink and be merry." Obviously his investments were such that he felt secure about his future. Like Belshazzar of Babylon, it was time to party! God's assessment of the farmer's security was not as gleeful. God said, "You fool! This night your soul will be required of you; then whose will those things be which you have provided?" The object lesson of our Lord warns us, none of our futures are secure if we lead a life that is so caught up in the security of materialism, that we forget God! (Luke 20:15-21).

The Money of the Lost

Jesus encourages us, "Do not worry, saying 'what shall we eat' or 'what shall we drink?' or 'what shall we wear?' for pagans run after all these things, and your heavenly Father knows that you need them" (Matthew 6:31-32 NIV). So why do people worry and fret over these things? Because they do not trust the Lord! They do not believe God is their source. Instead, they quote to themselves false scriptures, "The Lord helps those who help themselves." "He who has the gold, rules." All in an effort to justify there own covetous behaviors. Their pride demands that they keep up with the Jones. After all trusting God may only procure a used Civic, and one's self-esteem demands a new Prelude.

The Source of the Saved

The man whose heart is enlightened to God's

salvation, places his trust in the Lord, and behaves totally different with regard to his money. A regenerated man understands the giving nature of God, and knows there is no end to His provisions. He agrees with Paul who said, "He, who did not spare His own Son, but delivered Him up for us all, how shall He not with Him also freely give us all things?" (Romans 8:32). Because of God's heart, he works to earn a living and then freely gives to the Lord's purposes, knowing God's blessings will reward him. He rejects the workaholic lifestyle to spend time with his family and church, maintaining a balance in his life. Because the giving principle is divinely inspired, he knows God will honor all that obey. He wholeheartedly embraces Jesus' teaching, "Seek first the kingdom of God and His righteousness, and all these things shall be added to you" (Matthew 6:33). Therefore, he lives patiently, being content in the Lord, working diligently and allowing God to bring him the monetary blessings in the seasons of life as God chooses. Then he can rejoice over God's blessings with gratefulness, rather than patting himself on the back and boasting like Nebuchadnezzar, "It is by the might of my power."

Temptation to Compromise

After graduating from college with a degree in marketing, the job of corporate representative had just been offered to me. Now I was power munching with the Vice President and the National Sales Manager of the New York-Chicago based company. The waiter took our orders and served the mixed drinks to my new superiors, along with an ice tea for me. My new boss promptly leaned over and asked, "You do drink, don't you?" "Actually no," was my reply, anticipating my first sales lesson. "Well, if you will learn to nurse a beer, you will excel in acquiring business," stated my mentor. With youthful exuberance I blurted, "My God is much bigger than that, He fails at nothing and surely with His help I will be able to get plenty of business!" It's a wonder I wasn't promptly fired for my lack of diplomacy. I later learned to be much more discrete with my Christian values.

This story reminds me of two truths. First, *God's ways are successful*; I did become very proficient in sales by honoring God without discarding my values as a Christian. It was extremely challenging, but once the business community discovered I would tell the truth, and my word was my bond, they began to trust me with the responsibility of serving their needs. Secondly, *the world's way is compromise!* Business opportunities repeatedly presented themselves with concession tags. "My business for a case of beer each visit," said one buyer. Another requested a TV, another asked for a night with the company's secretary. One buyer even asked for local visits to the massage parlor in exchange for his business, "like the salesman before you," he announced!

The desire for wealth and pleasure are in constant conflict with our desire for God. Jesus warns of this temptation, "The cares of this world and deceitfulness of riches choke the word, and he becomes unfruitful" (Matthew 13:22). In other words, the more we yield ourselves to pleasure and money, the fainter our moral values become. The struggle to hang on to the moral high ground erodes with the rising tide of man's ambitions.

The American Dream of a Home!

After a short labor, our second son was born at 4AM.

The nurses encouraged me to go on home. My response was, "Well I have a home, but to be honest, wherever my wife is, that's my home, and I would like to stay with her and the infant to snuggle with them." To my surprise, they just marveled, and said it was the greatest compliment I could have paid my wife. The sentiment has never diminished! We now have six beautiful children and a wonderful home life.

The struggle has been difficult, in the early years of the ministry we filed tax returns exposing our poverty-level income. Actually, I thought we were doing okay. We were comfortable. We lived in a trailer and drove pre-owned cars. But after all those deductions, Uncle Sam reminded me that according to the median household incomes, we were living on the other side of the tracks. Eventually with hard work and patience, we bought a 25 year old, modest house and thought it was a mansion. We are slowly remodeling and my wife Linda exercises tremendous love, patience and sacrifice, giving it warmth and atmosphere. We've now paid it off and have live debt free for a good portion of our lives. As tempting as it has been through out the years, to have another income, it has been a tremendous blessing to have her stay at home, home schooling and raising the children. All of them are well adjusted and liked by their peers. It is the greatest feeling to come home after work and be met by my family at the door, in a day and age when men say it can't be done! These values were imparted to us by our parents' example.

Years ago when my father returned from WWII times where tough. As hard as they were, a man with a high school education could get a job, buy a house and provide for his family, without the spouse having to work. Now times have changed. Today it seems the American

Dream of having a home is a disaster. Often the husband and wife are college educated, working and struggling to make ends meet. The enormous financial pressures they place on themselves in order to have a home tear at the fragile seams of their marriage. Many say the economic pressures are due to inflation. I disagree.

When I look at my parents' quaint one bath, 900 square foot frame house I was born in, and the modest three bedroom, one bath, 1200 square foot, dream home I grew up in, I see a stark difference between then and now. Today, couples leverage their credit to the hilt, giving in to slick sales presentations of professionals who promise, "You can have it all!" Their homes start out with multiple baths, complete with Jacuzzis, saunas, his and her vanities and walk-in closets. The kitchen must be equipped with garbage disposals, trash compactors, microwaves, high-powered pot scrubbing dishwashers, and double ovens. The designer cabinets are made of the finest materials, suspended over Corian countertops. Beautiful burnished wood adorns the staircase, balcony and railings, towering over the polished radiance of hardwood floors. The house must have a fireplace, ceiling fans, chandeliers hanging in vaulted ceilings, smoke detectors and state of the art security systems. It is not complete without a double car garage with remote doors. The abode's furnishings duplicate the pictures of home decor magazines.

Payments on their late model cars add to their pressures, as they scamper off to work each morning with their bumper stickers displayed, "I owe, I owe, it's off to work I go!" On the way they drop off their toddlers at a day care that is conscientiously named, Preschool Learning Center, to remind them of society's approval of their pursuit of the American dream, to the demise of the love and attention their infants so desperately need.

To be honest, I don't get it! Why do people dart off to work at 5:30-6:30AM, work themselves delirious for careers requiring overtime till 7-8:00PM, Monday through Friday. Satisfying ungrateful bosses, so they can come home, catch a newscast, microwave dinner and tuck the children in, before they plop into bed exhausted, preparing to recycle the daily routine. Saturdays are spent manicuring the lawns, getting that home and garden curb appeal...that's if they're not in Aruba to scuba for the weekend getaway. All so they can sleep in on Sundays, get up and grab a cup of cappuccino, prop up their feet and read the paper and say, "How sweet it is?"

This is nothing more than covetousness, pride, and the vanity of materialism. What are they by example, teaching their children? Yesterday, to have a home was about love and relationship! But in today's world of success, love and family is subordinate to the materialistic home, reflecting pride, image and the perception of success. Their offspring will follow in the footsteps of their parents. The next generation will be poised to embrace any leader who can guarantee them an economic future better than their parents had.

The Commerce Day Parade

Mystery Babylon's spirit can be seen in a small borough that has been swallowed up by suburban sprawl. The district near my hometown has maintained its identity as a small town and become a magnet for young yuppie urbanites. Because of its affluence, the town is affectionately referred to as Mercedesville. Recently I attended their Christmas parade and it saddened me to see the virtual absence of any acknowledgment of Jesus

Christ from all the entries, with the exception of First Baptist Church's nativity scene and the United Pentecostal's banner, "I have seen the light!"

Perhaps the local municipality should instruct the sponsor, the Jaycees, if you are going to have a parade in the name of Christ, at least instruct the entries as to the meaning of a parade. Webster's dictionary defines parade as, "a public procession, to make a display or spectacle of." A foreigner leaned over during the parade and inquired, "Where is your Jesus?" What an embarrassment! This public spectacle had virtually nothing to do with the birth of a savior!

Just what is being taught to all those Indian, Tiger, Cub, and Boy Scout groups, dance clubs and marching bands? None of them visually or audibly expressed any reverence for Jesus Christ, nor did any of the businesses, which instead paraded their products and passed out flyers promoting their wares. What is being taught about Christmas to all the little children who came with their mommies and daddies? Is the mere shouting of "Merry Christmas" sufficient, when visually and audibly there is no reference to the true meaning of Christmas? The absence of exalting banners, floats and Christmas hymns renders the phrase impotent of any spiritual origin. Apparently the message is, "There is no room at the inn for Mary, Joseph and the baby Jesus."

Mercedesville is a great barometer of what is happening in communities all over America. It is time to awaken to the spiritual reality of what is being lost in the moral traditions of community character. Perhaps it would be a good idea for each parade entry to receive a reminder of the Christmas story along with their parade application, so they will remember what they are making a "display and spectacle of," as they walk with the public procession. I imagined the parade to be all of the civic groups extolling God for His gift of salvation through the miracle, virgin birth of Jesus Christ, making a public display and spectacle of the community's values and beliefs. If the community no longer embraces this long held tradition, then why not change the parade's name to reflect the reality of what they are doing, celebrating commerce. The passion of a community's spiritual character is revealed by their public observance of Christmas. Whether it is Mercedesville or the Rockefeller center, our country is losing its confession of Jesus Christ and turning to a profession of commerce, as it's almighty.

National Compromise

Mystery Babylon's spirit is intertwined with the present national debate over political fund raising. Can a politician really form policy without bias towards a corporation or foreign country that supported his campaign? The obvious answer is no! Despite their promises to reform the detrimental system of special interest pact money, they continue to spend vast amounts of time courting anyone with an open hand. Is this in the best interest of the country? Can government truly be pure in serving its people, when it sells the White House to domestic and foreign interests for personal and partisan political gain?

There has been much controversy over politicians winking at China's human rights violations. Why do they wink? Because of China's emerging capitalistic markets! The politicians compromise our long-standing ideal of respect for human rights, for the greater prospect of potential Chinese business for American corporations.

Totalitarian Revelation

During President Clinton's travels to China, much attention was given to the Tienanamen Square dissidents. These students were subjected to physical violence for the trespass of lifting up their voices against an oppressive government that could not give them such basic goods as toilet paper. Ten years later, the dissidents were individually interviewed concerning their former protests against the government. To my amazement, each interview shared a chorus of voices, now preoccupied with their capitalistic opportunities. Their previous passion had now evaporated in the face of an influx of western goods and personal business opportunities. They repeatedly pronounced the present government acceptable because it was delivering the goods. Now they have hope for a better future. But what about the oppressive nature of your totalitarian government they were asked? "As long as we keep our opinions to ourselves, there is no trouble," explained one dissident. These former dissidents have been seduced by Mystery Babylon's spirit.

My insight was illuminated to the present reality; *materialism is now valued more importantly than the individual right of free expression.* People are willing to compromise personal conviction to a murderous tyrant, if he can promise them economic prosperity. The emergence of a capitalistic market of over one billion people, one fifth of the world's population, who are willing to submit to a single leader, who has authority to execute with license, helps me to understand how the future Anti-Christ will convince the multitudes to embrace his economic mark in exchange for worship. Like the chinese ruler, the Anti-Christ will have the sovereignty to kill all that do not worship him

(Revelation13:15).　People　will　cooperate　with disingenuous reverence for the opportunity to buy and sell in the marketplace.

Jesus asked, "What will a man give in exchange for his soul?"　Like Esau of old, who exchanged his birthright for a bowl of soup, men will frivolously make the same eternal mistake.　Esau reasoned, "Behold I am at the point of death, what profit shall this birthright do for me?" (Genesis 25:29-34).　His estimation of spiritual inheritance was less than his desire for present gratification!　In the same way, people will reason, what good is the promise of salvation, I'll take the Anti-Christ's mark and prosper in the here and now!

Pocket Book Morals

Our values as a Christian nation are slowly eroding. And Mystery Babylon' spirit is taking America captive, as evidenced by our "pocket book" voting!　In the late seventies, President Carter was voted out in the midst of double-digit inflation, interest rates, and economic malaise.　In the late eighties, after the Gulf War, President Bush was riding the highest approval ratings in the history of the Presidency.　The economy began to slump, and in the following eighteen months Americans jumped in bed with an Arkansas Governor who was maligned as a result of integrity problems.　The people's mantra was, character doesn't matter.　The economy turned around and our country has enjoyed the best prosperity in decades.　Their choice for President however, has been rocked with unprecedented scandal. Illegal land deals yoked with hush money, tainted foreign campaign money and Oval office sex-capades had the ears of every American tingling.　Newscasts and talk shows were flippantly speaking of intimate sex acts so perverse, that many were asking their children to leave the living room. In the cover-up, the President lied to his wife, the cabinet, the grand jury and to us, the American people. Impeachment proceedings were voted on in light of our congressional laws, but the American people sent a strong message to Congress, by voting out the impeachment proponents and voting in the President's supporters in mid-term elections. In the late nineties, our message was loud and clear, keep that economy rolling.

Our Nation's moral principles of family, honesty, and character are now second place to our more highly esteemed values of jobs, money and prosperity. The decline of the Roman Empire was directly parallel to its abandonment of morals. Eventually, a foreign power invaded and conquered the mighty nation. America has no such threat. The Gulf War demonstrated that America's military is the best. Our borders are safe, but our yearning for materialism, money and economic opportunity has left our spiritual borders vulnerable to conquest. Is it possible, in the decline of our spiritual resolve, we will fulfill the Prophet John's vision of the Anti-Christ's world system, "These are of one mind, and will give their power and authority to the beast.... For God has put it into their hearts to fulfil his purpose, and to be of one mind, and give their kingdom to the beast, until the words of God are fulfilled" (Revelation 17:13+17). Emphatically, yes! Mystery Babylon will encompass Americans along with the rest of the nations, in the pursuit of economic freedom. Unwittingly, we will be ensnared by the devil, by joining the nations in the coming world market economy, controlled by the mark of the Anti-Christ. We will not be overpowered by a stronger nation, but instead by a spirit of covetousness' that will enslave us to Mystery Babylon.

Hail to the Chief...Federal Reserve Chairman

It used to be understood that our economy was susceptible to the policies of the governing body and of course they still are, long term. Now, huge swings on Wall Street's financial markets hinge on the demeanor, posture and gravity of every phrase spoken by the Federal Reserve Chairman. At each hint of change, enormous sums of money shift hands from one world market to another in search of more fertile investment yield. Each President's legacy hangs in the balance of the Federal Reserve Chairman's success at manipulating the interest rates to gain the financial result. Such power certainly hints at the possibility of a future world leader being trusted with enormous economic responsibility, especially if it is presented with the idea of mass stability, avoiding the volatility of fortunes lost.

Third World Yearnings

It has been my privilege to do the invocation and benediction for various dignitaries attending political events. Just to name drop a few, Senator Jesse Helms (head of the foreign relations committee), former Senator Lauch Faircloth of North Carolina and Senator Allan Simpson of Wyoming and Malcomb Baldridge, plus numerous governors, judges and state representatives.

On one such evening in the mid nineties, Presidential hopeful Steve Forbes was giving the keynote address. Forbes' presentation predicted the long and steady economic growth of America for several reasons. The cold war was over, and there was no need in light of the

Gulf War to keep pumping horrendous sums of money into the military. Secondly, third world nations were craving western goods that would provide a long and vast market for domestic corporations. Thirdly, because of communication technology, America was in a position to develop foreign business partners around the globe, marketing the wonders of western comforts and pleasures.

My short-term mission trips to third world countries have confirmed his global assessment. In Central America a little boy clasped my thigh and begged, "Please mister, please take me back to America with you." Why I asked? "So I can have Levis too," he cried. On another occasion, a young man who was fortunate to have access to a TV, asked me if all Americans were as rich as J. R. Ewing of Dallas fame.

In Asia, Uzbekistani students sang with fervency, "We are the World" in perfect English to welcome me to their school. When I asked them, why that song, they replied, "Oh, we memorized this one because it catches the eye of the United Nations officials and hopefully gets us more money."

One experience in particular gripped me. As we walked along the shore of a Caribbean island, my missionary friend picked up the remnants of a busted balloon. On it was the emblem of the "A Team." That evening as we shared the gospel of Jesus Christ, he asked the children to tell him the names of the "A Team." My thought was how would these little children, in this remote tropical village know who was on the "A Team?" To my amazement, they recited instantly every one of them. Then, he asked them for the names of the twelve disciples of Jesus. Sadly, they could not name a single one. My heart is filled with shame, as I realize the wealth of our nation in the eyes of the world, is not our faith and character, but instead our brand name jeans and Hollywood productions. Mystery Babylon's spirit lives on many waters, just as the prophet said.

Last Days, Perilous Times

"But know this, that in the last days perilous times will come: for men will be lovers of themselves, lovers of money, ...proud... without self control... haughty, lovers of pleasures rather than lovers of God...."

(2 Timothy 3:1-4).

What could possibly be wrong with desiring comfort and pleasure and how does that desire result in perilous times? After all, it was God who told His saints repeatedly that to eat, drink and enjoy the good of all our labor was the heritage that God gives to us. Solomon says all these things are a "gift from God" (Ecclesiastes 2:24, 3:13, 5:18-19). So what is wrong with desiring material pleasure? Nothing unless yearning for a thing is esteemed more than our love for God. This is why Mystery Babylon is described as, "THE MOTHER OF HARLOTS" ... with whom the inhabitants of the earth were made drunk with the wine of her fornication" (Revelation 17:2+5).

In the process of love making, there is a moment in foreplay when reason is cast off and emotion takes over. Many a teenager who became pregnant, explained themselves with this argument, "It was an accident, we didn't mean to go all the way, it just happened, we lost control, we didn't plan this...." Consider their argument. "It was an accident," they parked at the end of a long dark road and somehow climbed into the back seat. It was by chance they somehow took off each other's clothes and got naked. Their justification reveals an enormous truth about the power of lust over one's mental faculties. They simply lost all common sense in the face of unrestrained lust.

Like a dog in heat, finally ready to receive the advances of her lover, the world is reaching perilous *times*, ready to receive her Anti-Christ. Covetousness for money and pleasure will overshadow man's ability to rationalize his moral values. He will be seduced and commit fornication with the mother of all harlots, Mystery Babylon!

Chapter 4

Mystery Babylon's Search for Utopian Government!
"World Order through Buying and Selling"

"He causes all, both small and great, rich and poor, free and slave, to receive a mark on their right hand or on their foreheads, and that no one may buy or sell except one who has the mark...." Revelation 13:16-17

In 1988, my family moved to the rural edges of our community. There were lovely scenes of cows and horses grazing in the meadows, with hay bales waiting delivery to their barns. There was an old country store where farmers would gather at early morning breaks to tell their stories from the past, reminiscing while drinking sodas from antique six-ounce coke bottles and munching on nabs. Our house was located a mile farther down, just inside the woods off a dirt road. The church where I pastor is located seven miles away in the suburbs, and the short drive to my office was about fifteen minutes with only two traffic lights to negotiate.

Today, urban sprawl has taken over. Legions of subdivisions and apartment complexes have consumed the landscape. Strip malls serve the consumer's needs with groceries, pizza, hardware, videos, insurance, haircutting and fast food to name a few. Convenience stores are popping up with ATM's and gasoline. The dirt road is now asphalt and guiding DOT's estimated nine thousand cars per day to their destinations. Traffic is so bad they are building a second beltway around the city to help alleviate the congestion. Worst of all, my trip to the office is now hindered by numerous traffic lights.

Yellow Flashing Lights!

Each time the DOT installed traffic lights at another intersection, they would leave the yellow lights flashing for a short season. Yellow means to slow down and proceed with caution. The idea is to alert behaviorally conditioned drivers to the realization, that soon they will have to stop for a red light. They can not go barreling through the intersection as they have been conditioned too!

The scriptures give us numerous yellow flashing lights regarding the rise of Mystery Babylon. They are prophecies that warn us, proceed with caution in your present societal behaviors, for soon you will have to stop for the New World Order! The growth of mankind screams for government intervention to bring order to the chaos of society's burgeoning problems. This chaotic growth will be ultimately tamed by controlling man's buying and selling. The mark of the Anti-Christ will seek to accomplish this in Mystery Babylon.

Nebuchadnezzar's Utopian Government

The rise of Mystery Babylon is identical to the picture of Nebuchadnezzar's Babylon. The ancient ruler stepped onto the global stage by coalescing the kingdoms of the world into his domain. His last remaining insubordinates were those backsliding children of God, the Jews of Israel. Finally, after years of diplomacy he used brute force to conquer Jerusalem and take the people captive. There, dwelling under his domain they were required along with the rest of mankind to worship his golden image. To his dismay, the Jews who were pure in heart towards their God refused to worship his image, even in the face of death. His decision to persecute them by putting them to death in the fiery furnace resulted in the revelation of the Son of Man. What is recorded in the natural or historical events is a perfect picture of the spiritual or future events.

As we peer into the future I must confess, the individual details are as Paul said, "We see through a glass, darkly," for we "Know in part, and we prophecy in part...." (1 Corinthians 13:12). However, future events will unfold in Mystery Babylon, as they did in ancient Babylon. For the past is "Written for our admonition, on whom the ends of the ages have come" (1 Corinthians 10:11). It will not happen in the physical but it will happen in the spiritual.

The New World Order's Utopian Government

The present development of a universal personal identification code (UPIC) tells us something about our society. Sophisticated corporate marketing only seeks to supply a product, *if there is demand.* For the foundation of all free market economies is supply and demand. So obviously there is a demand!

But demand from whom? One possible answer may be in the development of third world countries. The astronomical growth of society, both domestically and abroad in emerging markets like China, beg for control and management, much like the busy intersections and urban sprawl discussed above. An interesting news story appeared on the evening news, "Third world countries are being taught by the IRS how to collect taxes." The yearnings of these countries to supply their citizens with the luxuries of western lifestyle demand they learn how to collect revenue to fund the development of utilities, highways and infrastructure. Without some method of identifying their citizens, they are powerless to raise funds much the same way the IRS is impotent to audit you without a social security number. If you are not in the computer, you don't exist! Besides, what good is a Lexus if you don't have a smooth asphalt road to drive?

The United Nation's development of third world countries into a New World Order will absolutely require some form of successful taxation similar to America's IRS and social security card. This vision will not be successful with national promises to contribute to the welfare of the UN, as evidenced by the UN's constant complaining about present delinquent countries. Some young visionary will possibly observe the successful test market use of the implanted microchip and begin persuading the nations of the world to adopt its usage to accommodate a uniform system that all can grow into. Or it may be an exclusive idea promoted by the UN to lure the nations into an economic coalition.

"Why should we?" will be the natural objection of third world countries. The answer lies in the success of government legislation, such as NAFTA. Such strokes of the legislative pen have opened up markets for greater commerce and free trade among the participating nations. They did it to keep from falling behind in the growth of their gross national product (GNP) or free enterprise. As a result, their economies continued to grow to the benefit of their people.

Another example of the demand for common economic ground is the present push for the Euro, Europe's parallel to the American dollar. Any tourist knows the present system is archaic. In the late nineties I passed through numerous European countries and found myself stuffing their individual currencies into different pockets. The English pound was in the front right pocket of my blue jeans. The German mark was in my left-hand pocket. The French frank was in my back left, along with my wallet, while the Italian lira was in the other back pocket. When I got to Belgium, and went to purchase a soda, my whole organization collapsed. The cashier asked for the money and it wasn't in the front or back. Finally I began pulling out everything and asked if she saw any of her money in the pile!

Undoubtedly, once the bugs are worked out the uniform Euro will propel the Confederated States of Europe to being one of the greatest markets on the face of the earth. It will be a shining example of how to keep up economically. No doubt, this and other mergers will create an atmosphere of cooperation to stay in touch with the monetary pulse of the emerging global market.

Another possible venue of persuasion will be the success of China's government to bring in capitalism. The argument will be, hey ...you want peace with your people, you want them to stop fighting and rebelling, then give them what they want, hope for the future. Give them free access to the marketplace, to jobs, and it will give them opportunity, something to do with all their idle time. They will be happier and less preoccupied with how to overthrow the government. In addition, you can still run a totalitarian dictatorship if you want! Here lies the timelessness of Solomon's wisdom, "Oppression makes a wise man mad, and a gift destroys his heart" (Ecclesiastes 7:7).

Still another will be the use of opportunity grants. The American government has used this to tremendous advantage with the most favored nation status. This is the way it works, if you cooperate with their ideals and don't give them any hassle, they will trade with you by putting you highest on the priority trading list. It also means foreign grants and monetary supports. The United Nations uses the same principle with the International Monetary Fund (IMF). If they like you, economic opportunities abound, there will be no trade sanctions against you, and if you get into financial trouble, they will be there to bail you out. Again, Solomon's wisdom speaks loudly, "It is wrong to accept a bribe to twist justice" (Proverbs 17:23). Bribes are morally wrong, but it is done universally. Like the pied piper, the children of the nations will follow the money to their utopian world government.

All of these emerging capitalistic markets will desire to improve their ability to tax their citizens and maintain a competitive economic edge in the world marketplace. The universal personal identification code (UPIC) will facilitate their governing the masses, by enhancing their ability to tax and equalizing access to the marketplace. All these events and more will enable a young politician to rise from obscurity to a position of assembling the nations into a world agreement centered on a cooperative system of commerce (Revelation 13:16-17 + 17:12-13).

The Internet

The embryo of the world marketplace is already sweeping the globe via the Internet. On-line buying and selling is escalating as safety measures to protect fraud are implemented. Information is available immediately. This aspect alone is revolutionizing marketing from supply and demand to demand and supply. What is the difference? Personal scanners are being developed to allow people to scan any bar code and immediately find out who sells the product at the lowest price. People simply identify themselves as a buyer, (in search of a particular product) and sellers come running to supply. This kind of competition will eventually drive prices so low, that in order to compete a retailer or merchant must join the global network. And if you want more and more, you can get it for less and less by connecting to the system. The unrestrained covetousness of the multitudes will demand their governments conform, to give them access to the best deals possible.

Retailers and consumers using PC's will connect globally via the World Wide Web. Ultimately a computer chip in your right hand will access the web, while eliminating the threat of fraud through identity theft. Your power to purchase will either be debited or credited, as you're online transactions are recorded and compiled in massive databases. Eventually, when all this technology comes to full maturity and worldwide saturation, it will become mandatory that everyone participates. Each national government will subscribe by doing away with national currency, making it impossible to buy and sell without the universal personal identification code (UPIC).

666

There is much discussion over the number six, six, six! I have heard of people who use esoteric Hebrew numerology to calculate each president's name, looking for hidden Hebrew meanings and insight to the coming Anti-Christ.

I once suggested to Joseph Woodlake, the inventor of the UPC symbol (bar code) for IBM, that it appeared the computer was tabulating information from the three bands in the bar code: left, center and right. Each band seem to match the band for the number six on the left side of the code, giving the governing principle to the bar code of six, six, six. Mr. Woodlake scoffed at my suggestion, pointing out that the laser did not read numbers, instead it only read bands of light and darkness. I insisted that the governing bands (left, center, and right) were identical to the left side band numbered six, for human comprehension. He retorted, "That's impossible, because the right side is the mirror image of the left side, therefore whatever is light is now dark, and whatever is dark is now light. The laser does not read numbers; it only reads contrasts of light and darkness. Therefore the band on the right side that represents a six is a mirror reflection of the left side band that represents a six and therefore does not match the three governing bands (left, center and right)." Are you confused? At this point, you are probably totally confused and admittedly, it is difficult to understand in layman's terms.

Bar Code's Light Paradox

Who am I to tell Mr. Woodlake how it functions? After all, he invented it. He should know. However, I discern one thing. The UPC symbol and the subsequent universal personal identification code (UPIC) are a reflection of the times. When in the history of humanity has man ever bought and sold with anything but hard currency or barter? *Never!* When the UPIC microchip is implemented, this single monetary unit of exchange, when substituted for cash will clearly reveal the prophetic truth of God and the imminent return of Jesus Christ! Unfortunately, when the mark is implemented, the multitude will rush to embrace it and it will be to their spiritual demise.

Oh yes, by the way, Isaiah cried, "Woe to them...who say, 'Let God hurry, let him hasten His work so we may see it... **Let the plan of the Holy One of Israel come**, so we may know it...who call evil good and good evil, **who put darkness for light and light for darkness"** (Isaiah 5:18-20 NIV). The Apostle John wrote, "This calls for wisdom. If anyone has insight, let him calculate the number of the beast, for it is man's number. His number is 666" (Revelation 13: 18 NIV).

God is light and rebellion is darkness. The machine does not read numbers as we do. To the laser scanner, light and darkness have no moral value. Its technology is a reflection of man's incredible ingenuity and unfortunately, a symbol of man's amoral heart in these last days.

The number six in Biblical numerology always represents man. Especially in the context of rebellion and trusting in his own efforts to the exclusion of God. Man was created on the sixth day, six days were allotted to man for work in a week and Hebrew law said a servant must serve for six years to obtain his freedom. The number six magnified, such as six, six, six, is merely the culmination of man's wisdom regarding his ability to gain wealth and financial independence. The beast's 666 expresses man's attempt to finally arrive at earthly utopia, to the exclusion of God.

The Anti-Christ's Sign: Peace or Mark?

For years people said the Anti-Christ would be whoever made peace with Israel. Recent events of the last decade record many that have made peace with Israel. President Jimmy Carter orchestrated it first with Israel's

Prime Minister Menachan Began and Egypt's Anwar Sadat. Then there was President Bush with Israel's Prime Minister Rabin and Palestine's Arafat. Then King Hussien of Syria signed on. Then President Clinton with Israel's Prime Minister Netanyahu and Palestine's Arafat made peace again.

Frankly, I believe whoever convinces the nations to join the world market system in which no man might buy or sell without the mark is the Anti-Christ. This is the sign we should be looking for. He will no doubt sell the nations on the question, what are we fighting for anyway, we can all have our cake and eat it too by jumping on the prosperity wagon. The sixties' wisdom of "make love, not war" will give way to "make wealth, not war." Consider the ramifications of this powerful little microchip that will appear as a small mark in the right hand or forehead.

The Anti-Christ will have absolute power to tax, probably through a world sales tax on every monetary transaction. He will then give back to individual countries pork barrel money to invest in their development.

The Anti-Christ will have absolute control over every human being on the face of the planet. People will seek to stay in his good graces, for it would be a terrible thing to walk into a grocery store and find out access to your account is denied.

The Anti-Christ will be able to trace your every movement via global positioning satellites, or by monitoring the flow of transactions linked to the microchip in your hand. If he suspects you are buying terrorist propaganda and are purchasing guns and ammunitions, you may well receive a knock at your door from the local authorities.

The Anti-Christ will virtually eliminate black market commodities such as cocaine, marijuana, or stolen properties, unless of course the criminal element transfers funds via computer. Crime will take a hit. What does the thief steal, certainly not cash?

The whole concept of being powerless to buy the essentials of life such as food, electricity, cars, gasoline, telephone or water is a powerful inducement to comply with his wishes. He will easily take the nations of the world captive, much like Nebuchadnezzar of ancient Babylon.   The old adage, absolute power, corrupts absolutely, will take on a whole new realm of meaning. Like Nebuchadnezzar's golden image, it will be "dejavu." After all, he who has the gold rules.

The ambitious politician who implements all of this may very well be just that, an ambitious politician seeking to improve the livelihood of mankind. But unwittingly, he falls into the diabolical scheme of Satan. The new adage of Lucifer will be, absolute power to let buy and sell, will surely send them all to hell (Revelations 14:9-11).

For Christians, we need to live a lifestyle as the Apostle John said, "Do not love the world, or the things in the world. If anyone loves the world, the love of the Father is not in him. For all that is in the world-the lust of the flesh, the lust of the eyes, and the pride of life-is not of the Father but is of the world. And the world is passing away, and the lust of it; but he who does the will of God abides forever" (1 John 2:15-17). This daily discipline will allow God's character to establish itself firmly within us. So in that day and hour we are prepared to join Shadrach, Meshach and Abednego in saying to Nebuchadnezzar, "We will not serve your gods, nor worship the golden image, which you have set up" (Daniel 3:18).

Unfortunately, there were many Jews in Babylon during that hour of trial and temptation. The prophet records only a few who were willing to "Love not their lives, even unto death" (Revelation 12:11). In the next chapter, we will see how the Anti-Christ begins to subdue the backslidden children of God and take them away captive, just as Nebuchadnezzar took the Jews in ancient Babylon.

Chapter 5

The Captivity of Mystery Babylon!
"The Great Falling Away"

"That Day will not come unless the falling away comes first, and the man of sin is revealed, the son of perdition." 2 Thessalonians 2:3

The Apostle Paul says the coming of the Lord is signaled by a falling away of many from the faith, and the revealing of the Anti-Christ.   In chapter four, the pinpoint evidence of the Anti-Christ's identity, has to do with the one who coalesces the nations into a world agreement concerning buying and selling, and implements with enforcement the mark of the beast. This will be a huge challenge and will encompass the persuasive powers of covetousness, money and pleasure. These cunning powers prey on carnality and will have the combined effect of causing the anemic faith of many to fall by the way side and succumb to the pressure of taking the mark, as illustrated by the Irish boy.

The Irish Boy

A rugged young lad in front of me at the check out line had just gotten a new tattoo on his left arm. The immediate skin around the brilliant colors was still puffy. Intrigued, I asked him about the process of being tattooed and especially why he chose the three leaf clover.
"Oh it is the Irish symbol," he quipped!
Pondering, I inquired, "Isn't the luck of the Irish a four leaf clover?"

"No, no," the youthful lad laughed, enlightening me, "The three leaves are the Father, the Son, and the Holy Ghost."

"Oh, I didn't know, well you must be born again," I rejoiced.

"No, but I know all about being saved," he declared, moving forward in the line, "my whole family is very religious."

"Well, what are you waiting for," I pressed, "if you know the truth of Jesus, what keeps you from receiving salvation today?"

Exchanging the cash for the six-pack and Joe camels, he retorted, "It's not the year 2000 yet and I got some living to do. I will, but not yet!"

This man's heart was very honest and it exposed the rationale undergirding many people's faith. It says, "I want to party and live for the flesh, but I also want to go to heaven. So knowing the time is short, I'll turn to the Lord by the year 2000, because Christ may come back for us soon." The Irish boy misunderstood the marvelous personal relationship we receive in knowing Jesus as Lord and instead settled for spiritual fire insurance, just in case the rapture comes. This young lad's faith can not possibly be representative of the Christian who is "without spot or blemish" (Ephesians 5:27), that the Apostle Paul said Jesus would be coming for when He returns.

Millennium Hopes

A number of years ago a book was written, *"Eighty-eight reasons why the Lord will return in 1988."* The book was so well distributed; the media picked up on it and did news stories of Christians expecting the rapture. I still remember the frenzy of excitement demonstrated by numerous Christians, as they prepared themselves for the Lord's return. I also remember the displeasure they felt towards me for not embracing their hope. It was almost as if they thought if you don't believe this, you won't go when the rapture happens! I also remember the dismay, discouragement and embarrassment they felt in January of 1989. Plus, secular people chided the Christian community for yet another false exploitation of hope.

Are you ready for a repeat? The year 2000 has had many Christians buzzing for several decades. Many were convinced of the year, while others are focused on a brief time frame of several years after the year 2000. Again the media is picking up on it. National tabloids are proclaiming so-called Bible prophecies, Nostradamus and misquotations of Rev. Billy Graham, to add credibility. All of this will fuel the exploitation of false hope and repeat the net effect of dismay, discouragement and embarrassment.

Each passing year will increase the taunts of the unsaved and the anemic faith of those like the Irish boy will collapse in the face of their ridicule. Bewildered, they will return to their carnal living joining in heart with the chorus of the scoffers, "Where is the promise of His coming...all things continue as they were from the beginning...." (2 Peter 2:4).

The Mark and the Utopian Dream

As the years pass and turn-of-the-millennium concerns fade, the social architects will begin to focus on constructing the utopian society. Eventually, ideas including the implanted microchip will go from speculative rumor to broader discussion. Finally, technocrats will envision the universal personal identification code (UPIC) as the convergent solution to society's development. Just as the Euro has been debated, discussed, examined and re-examined for alternative solutions before proceeding, so it will be with the microchip technology. Moreover, just like the Israel/Palestine peace accord is slowly plodding along towards a future treaty, the microchip technology (UPIC) will take decades of discussion before international legislative pens ever strike an agreement.

During that season of time, fear of the unknown will begin to fade, as people are enlightened to the ease of access the implanted micro-chip will bring in the marketplace. They will be promised new lines of credit, no more banking as usual, or cash to grapple with, no more check writing, or monthly bill paying, just instantaneous drafts of their microchip access accounts. The promise will be faster and more efficient service with no more lines to wait in and a host of other incentives.

Each of society's cultures will begin to endorse the microchip with futuristic optimism as media coverage increasingly erodes consumer resistance. Christians will be chided for their Neanderthal ways and reluctance to grasp the future. It will no longer be, "this is the nineties," instead it will be, "this is the twenty-first century!" Bible-believing Christians will be disparaged in comparison to other major religions' progressive acceptance, as Hindus, Muslims, and Jews sign on. The future peer pressure can be illustrated by a humorous personal dilemma I discovered called the "microscope of peer pressure."

The Microscope of Peer Pressure

At sporting events, I always watch with amusement during the halftimes, the long lines waiting to use the women's restroom. "Why is that," I ask my wife. "Because it takes so much longer for women to use a stall," replies the bride. She then marvels that men can line up on a wall and do our business in full sight of everyone. "Oh, no problem," I boast, "There is plenty of room for everyone and nobody is looking."

To my chagrin, my glorying broke down at a recent church conference. It was standing room only at the mega church, when finally we were released for the potty break. Both lines to the men and women's restrooms were long. Patiently waiting, I kept thinking, what is taking so long? As precious time ticked away, I finally reached the bathroom door. Peering inside I could see the guys lined up around the wall. Gradually, inching forward and now standing just inside the door, I could see two urinals being aggressively sought after. As each one became available, the line would shift down the wall and watch, as each patron would stand over the urinal endlessly.

I kept thinking as the bladder pressure was mounting, what's wrong with these guys, get on with it, nobody takes this long to relieve themselves. Finally, I'm on deck and baby I'm ready. As I settled into position over the porcelain fixture, abruptly I sensed the eyes of all those men on my back. Suddenly the urge vanished. I felt nothing. Nothing but the earnest desire to zip up and get out, pronto! Who needs this? Then the mental anguish of reality set in. If I walk out that door without seizing my opportunity, the urge will return with haste and I will be full of remorse. Suddenly, I found myself concentrating as never before, blocking out everything but the task at hand, and wrestling with the image of all those guys against the wall wondering, what is taking so long? Relax, I thought, as I gathered my poise, until at last I was humming "O victory in Jesus!"

Have you ever-felt peer pressure? In similar fashion, the gaze of the world will be fastened on Christians as they are maligned and denigrated for rebelling against the optimism of the futuristic microchip economy (UPIC). It will require spiritual fortitude to stand by your inner convictions under their microscope. Unfortunately, many halfhearted Christians will fall away during this season. Why, what would cause men to relinquish to their reasoning, and turn away from the hope of God?

The Covetous Captives

The answer lies in the Old Testament prophets. They foretold the Israelites of the impending invasion of Nebuchadnezzar for decades and their eventual bondage to Babylon. But they would not listen! They thought to themselves, Jerusalem is a fortified city with strong walls; on a hilltop making it virtually impossible to defeat. No one is going to come in here and take us captive. Accordingly, they vanquished any thoughts of future captivity and went on their merry way, buying and selling. Ezekial said about their heart attitude, in the face of impending Babylonian captivity, "My people...hear your words, but they will not do them: for with their mouths they show much love, but their heart goes after covetousness" (Ezekial 33:31). The prophets repeatedly warned the Jews of the impending judgment for their covetous ways (Jeremiah 2:23, 6:11-13, 17:5, 22:13-17,

48:7, 49:4 Ezekial 12:13, 22:13, Isaiah 30:28). It was all
to no avail, for they refused to repent and turn back to the
Lord.   In fact, they got so tired of hearing about the
coming judgment, they began to say among themselves,
"The days go by and every vision comes to nothing"
(Ezekial 12:22). Likewise, Peter forewarned in the New
Testament of the secular world's mantra, "Where is the
promise of His coming? For...all things continue as they
were from the beginning" (1 Peter 3:4).

The prophets even reprimanded them for their lazy
attitude toward the Sabbaths (Ezekial 20:20-24+30,
22:8+26). Today it is the same. I once read a survey that
said 86% of Americans believe in God. This is their
confession, but on Sunday mornings they are lazy. I do
not see the same traffic congestion on Sunday mornings
as I do on Monday, when everyone is driving to work to
earn more greenbacks labeled, "In God We Trust." The
Department of Transportation will tell you the slowest
traffic time of the week is Sunday morning. This is a
pathetic indictment of the spiritual condition of America,
land of the free and home of the brave. The truth is, "with
our mouths we show much love, but our hearts go after
covetousness."   Our actions cry loud and clear, in
Washington, Lincoln, Hamilton, Jackson, Grant and
Franklin we trust.

Like the Jews who were led away captive by
Nebuchadnezzar, the covetous will be spiritually led
away by the Anti-Christ's persuasions. Jesus admonished
the Laodicean Church saying, "Because you are
lukewarm...I will spew you out of my mouth. Because
you say, 'I am rich, have become wealthy, and have need
of nothing'-and do not know that you are wretched, poor,
blind, and naked- I counsel you to buy from me gold
refined in the fire, that you may be rich; and white

garments, that you may be clothed, that the shame of your nakedness may not be revealed; anoint your eyes with eye salve, that you may see" (Revelation 3:16-20). Jesus is chastening His saints, like a coach with a half-time deficit in the score. Come on, get with it, get serious about this game, quit being lazy and lethargic and lets get on the ball, play like you mean it! Jesus described this slothful spiritual relationship to God this way, "They say they are Jews and are not, but lie...." (Revelation 3:9).

What happened to the Jews in historical Babylon is the same thing that will happen to the spiritually lazy in Mystery Babylon. They will be taken captive because their covetous hearts made them drunk, unable to walk straight or see correctly. These people will be members of denominations who sporadically attend church. They will be prosperous neighbors; co-workers and relatives who acknowledge Christ, but in reality are trusting money. Jesus is exhorting us to the reality of two different kinds of riches. One is rich with materialism to the exclusion of God and the other is rich in spiritual character, willing to exclude materialism if need be.

The False Prophets

Amazingly, false prophets encouraged the backsliding Jews in their covetous lifestyle. Unlike Isaiah, Jeremiah or Ezekial, some false prophets were not interested in any awkward confrontations. It was much easier to speak the words the people wanted to hear and avoid any persecution from the majority persuasion. Ezekial records, "Woe unto the foolish prophets, that follow their own spirit, and have seen nothing. Because with lies, you...have strengthened the hands of the wicked, that he should not return from his wicked way, by promising him

life" (Ezekial 13:3+22). Likewise Paul warned Timothy,
"The time will come when they will not endure sound
doctrine, but according to there own desires, because they
have itching ears, they will heap up for themselves
teachers; and they will turn their ears away from the truth,
and be turned aside unto fables" (2 Timothy 4:3-5).

Ezekial said the spiritual shepherds of his day, "fed
themselves...not my flock" (Ezekial Chapter 34). Isaiah
and Jeremiah echoed Ezekial's sentiments (Isaiah 9:15-16
Jeremiah 26:8-11). At last Isaiah predicted they would go
into Babylonian captivity because, "They regard not the
work of the Lord...therefore my people are gone into
captivity, because they have no knowledge" (Isaiah 5:12-
13). It is interesting that Isaiah said they *had* gone into
captivity, using the past tense to describe a future event.
He is simply saying the covetousness spirit of Mystery
Babylon already has you in bondage, and you are
powerless to break it, because you do not seek the Lord.
Jesus is not your first love, money is!

Astonishingly, Jeremiah speaks an interesting truth,
"The prophets prophesy falsely, and ...my people love to
have it so" (Jeremiah 5:31). Why would people not want
to know the truth? Jeremiah again observed their human
carnality, "The heart is deceitful, above all things and
desperately wicked: who can know it?" (Jeremiah 17:9).
The people did not understand their own heart; they
simply lusted after materialism. Like the teenager void of
understanding how she became pregnant, the answer lies
in the reality that lust overcomes our ability to think
rationally. Jesus made the same comment about His
generation when He said, "Wisdom is justified by all her
children" (Matthew 11:19). This means that whatever
people choose to believe; they will somehow find a way
to validate it as truth, regardless of its absurdity. Just

look at the evolutionist's insistent conviction despite the absence of Darwin's transitional fossils. Now they make a mockery of God's Word by putting feet on the Christian fish symbol and replacing the name of Jesus with Darwin.

The Bottomless Pitfall of Prosperity

Two decades ago, the Holy Spirit gave a tremendous revelation to the church about God's prosperity. I say amen! Anyone turning to God is going to come out of poverty and begin to prosper. Unfortunately, today we have churches built around the over emphasis of the doctrine of prosperity. The prosperity doctrine has given way to a myriad of Christians who desire to get independently wealthy, but in reality, they pursue wealth to the exclusion of a committed church life. This lifestyle has subverted God's original purpose to bless their lives. Without repentance, nothing will change in the future.

God does not need our money. He wants our obedience! If we can't be faithful in attending church and paying our tithes now, what makes us think in the future anything will change. We have already made our decision to take the mark each time we roll over in bed and say to ourselves, next week I'll go to church. Each time the tithing plate passes and we rationalize, I'll be able to give abundantly in the near future, we say yes to the spirit of Mystery Babylon and are in captivity now! Just as the prophet Isaiah spoke past tense of Israel's Babylonian captivity before they were taken, so are lazy Christians already captive to Mystery Babylon before the microchip mark is implemented.

Jesus forewarned the spirit of these last days saying, "Many false prophets will rise up and deceive many. And because lawlessness will abound, the love of many will grow cold. But he who endures to the end shall be saved" (Matthew 24:11-13). God's law is the only true law. Most middle and upper class Americans would not dream of breaking the eighth commandment, "You shall not steal," or the sixth command, "You shall not kill," or even the ninth command "You shall not lie." Yet they think nothing of breaking the fourth command, "Remember the Sabbath day to keep it Holy," or the tenth command, "You shall not covet." It is this abounding lawlessness of materialism called covetousness that causes us to slack off in church attendance and when we do visit, our gift to God is no more than the tip we give the waitress at the restaurant. No wonder our love for the Lord and His church has grown cold.

We need to shake ourselves and repent, or we will be caught up in the falling away, justifying ourselves as we go. Paul wrote Timothy, warning him of men, "Quibbling over the meaning of Christ's words and stirring up arguments ending in jealousy and anger...their minds warped by sin...to them the Good News is just a means of making money...For the love of money is the first step toward all kinds of sin. Some people have even turned away from God because of their love for it, and as a result have pierced themselves with many sorrows" (1 Timothy 6:4-5+10 TLB). Like Demas who forsook the Apostle Paul, "having loved this present world," we live on the spiritual edge of joining the beast in the bottomless pit, if we personally accept the mark.

Wealth before God

Consider the story of the rich young ruler. Jesus did not deny that he had kept all the commandments from his youth up, however, He did discern that he had a problem with the priority of his wealth. In answer to his question, "What must I do to inherit eternal life," Jesus instructed him to "Sell all he had and distribute to the poor, and come and follow Me." What a marvelous invitation, the same invitation Jesus offered to the other twelve disciples. Had he obeyed, we could very well be reading the gospel according to the rich young ruler, but sadly he went away very sorrowful...for he was very rich. Jesus responded to his sad countenance by saying, "How hard it is for those who have riches to enter the kingdom of God. It is easier for a camel to go through the needle's eye, than for a rich man to enter the kingdom of God" (Luke 18:18-27). It is not impossible, but it does require tremendous humility to kneel before God like that camel crawling through the gate of Jerusalem called "the eye of the needle." This kind of Godly reverence and fear will be needed if we are going to rise above the Anti-Christ's indecent proposal of going to bed with the mother of harlots for the security of future wealth. All of our righteousness will not help us in that pivotal moment of decision if we love our money more than God.

The scriptures speak loud and clear; "Do you not know that the unrighteous will not inherit the kingdom of God? Do not be deceived. Neither fornicators, nor idolaters, nor adulterers, nor homosexuals, nor sodomites, nor thieves, nor **covetous**, ...will inherit the kingdom of God (1 Corinthians 6:10). What is God saying? Any of these things have the potential to lead us into damnation. Covetousness will do that by causing us to receive the mark of the beast. The Achilles' heel of middle and upper class America is the temptation to believe our beautiful homes, cars and mutual funds, are somehow security blankets. We never say it, but we certainly live it. We are, "Men of corrupt minds, and destitute of the truth, supposing that gain is godliness," just as Paul said (1 Timothy 6:5). We have a great need to repent of our lifestyles, it is time to spiritually grow up and put away our childish security blankets and turn to God who can teach us that, "Godliness with contentment is great gain. For we brought nothing into this world and it is certain we can carry nothing out" (1Timothy 6:6-7). These are the true riches of God, born of character that only comes from dying to self and living for Christ.

The Marriage Supper of the Lamb!

Consider another parable of Jesus. The great supper was extended to all that were invited saying come, for all things are ready. Nevertheless, they all began to make excuses. And they were good apologies. One had just bought some real estate, another acquired a business, and the last a new marriage. We use these same justifications today, to justify ourselves as too busy to attend church. However, in the parable, the master was angry and deplored; "None of those men who were invited shall taste of my supper" (Luke 14:15-24). Jesus was making an emphatic declaration of God's assessment of the latter days when men will choose the mark, to maintain their worldly pursuits. But to Christians, who decide to trust God for a seat at the parallel, marriage supper of the Lamb, he declares to be "blessed!" (Revelation 19:7-9).

Finally, the Apostle Paul warns, "The Spirit expressly says that in latter times some will depart from the faith, giving heed to deceiving spirits and doctrines of demons...having their own conscience seared with a hot iron" (1 Timothy 4:1-2). Mystery Babylon is a seducing spirit and Satan himself motivates the Anti-Christ. Together they will have seductive powers to convince the world to receive the mark, the tiny little microchip, that Jesus described as, "The hour of trial, which shall come upon the whole world, to test those who dwell on the earth" (Revelation 3:10+14:9-12).

It will be a defining moment in which each Christian will truly have to gather himself and trust in the Lord. He must focus on the task at hand, to simply rest in the Lord by refusing the gaze of a godless world. And vow not to accept the new implanted microchip technology.

Chapter 6

Mystery Babylon's Nebuchadnezzar
"The Anti-Christ"

"Little children, it is the last hour; and as you have heard that the Anti-Christ is coming...by which we know that it is the last hour." 1 John 2:18

Unfortunately, the son of perdition does not come with political yard signs, exclaiming, *"Vote for me, my platform is anti Christ!"* Instead, like a classic mystery novel, clues confirm our suspicions until we finally come to the truth of who done it. We may not know the murderer's name. However, if we are told it is a bitter servant who was nixed from the will for the reappearance of a long-lost illegitimate son, we have at least narrowed the suspect down to the domestic help. That he had the physical strength to smother the rich benefactor in the middle of the night eliminates the maid for her petite bone structure and the chauffeur who is only on call during the day. Focus now rests on the butler who is frequently seen with a towel draped over his arm, until the autopsy reports a chicken bone in the deceased throat was planted to help cover the crime. Suddenly the chef is a prime suspect, until we find out he was out of town until dawn. Finally, the micro fibers of the towel at the scene of the crime and under the butler's finger nails link him to the despicable act, especially since his debit card reveals he had dinner at the "Chicken Palace" the evening of the murder. The butler did it!

Likewise the Anti-Christ is revealed by emerging clues. Though we don't know his name, we do know that he is the one who ultimately gathers the nations of the world into a uniform government. In addition, he seeks to control world citizens with a mark on their right hand or forehead, so that no one might buy or sell without it. In appendix A there are fifty plus scriptural clues to the Anti-Christ. In this chapter, we will discuss only nine.

Clue #1   Deception by Any Means, the Coming Revolution

The Apostle Paul warns us about the timing of our gathering unto the Lord. He says, "Let no one deceive you by any **means**; for that Day will not come unless the falling away comes first, and the man of sin is revealed, the son of perdition" (2 Thessalonians 2:3). The Greek word translated **means**, is "tropos" (pronounce trop'os). Its meaning is *mode, or style of character.* It comes from the root word "trope" (pronounce trop-ay') which means *to turn or revolution.* The revealing of the Anti-Christ is yoked with a change in public opinion, induced by the charisma of a politician who has "par excellence" in persuading the masses to his viewpoint, resulting in social revolution.

The French Revolution is a lesson in the behavioral pattern of the carnal heart. Alex de Tocqueville warned his fellow countrymen of the attempt to govern a nation without the support of religion. The Age of Reason was in full bloom, a period where society was casting off the restraints of the Catholic Church and embracing Atheism. When Queen Marie Antoinette offended the masses with her famous comment, "Let them eat cake," the starving masses were easily rallied to full rebellion under the leadership of Maximilien Robespierre. Their desire was to overthrow the wealthy aristocrats and establish a social equality. The guillotine was used proficiently as a tool of persuasion.

Today, the same dynamics are germinating worldwide. The present reasoning of carnal men, is one of casting off the church in exchange for seeking pleasure. In addition, the third world masses yearn for equality with America's lifestyle. Like a dry forest vulnerable to a single match, the world is awaiting its next Robespierre to lead them in the revolution, hungering for materialistic equality to the exclusion of God.

Clue #2   Context of Peace and Flatteries

The Anti-Christ's persuasive flatteries in the coming decades will put the crowning touches on a revolution that has already begun in our present political arena. Supreme Court Justice Clarence Thomas once declared, "It used to be racism was directed toward the color of your skin: today racism is directed toward the ideology of your heart." As we have discussed, the majority of Americans now have morals that are rooted in their pocket books, rather than our founding fathers' Christian values. Because of the seduction of materialism, the Anti-Christ will render the Christian ideology impotent. The saints desire to persuade the public to resist the implementation of his mark will not be able to stop his plan according to John's thirteenth chapter of Revelation.

The desire of the nations to have full access to the economic opportunities of the future will make them vulnerable to all of the Anti-Christ's flatteries (Daniel 11:32). He will tell people anything that they want to hear in order to gain power. He will promise world peace for all that sign on to the global economic agreement. But sudden destruction will be coming from the Lord as judgment on all who reject God in accepting the Anti-Christ's plan (Daniel 11:21, 1Thessalonians 5:3).

Clue #3   Coalition of the Nations

The Apostle John foretells of the Anti-Christ's ability to assemble Mystery Babylon's global union. "Power was given to him over all kindred, and tongues, and nations...These have one mind, and shall give their power and authority to the beast... For God hath put it in their hearts to fulfill His will, and to agree, and give their kingdoms unto the beast, until the words of God shall be fulfilled" (Revelation 13:7 17:13+17 KJV).

In like manner, Nebuchadnezzar of ancient Babylon required all of the "Princes, the governors, and the captains, the judges, the treasurers, the counselors, the sheriffs, and all the rulers of the provinces, to come to the dedication of the image which Nebuchadnezzar the king had set up." After all, he was the head of gold and God had given him dominion over the whole earth (Daniel 2:38 3:2 4:2).

But the key is, God is the one who grants these men their power and authority. God is ending the present world system and forcing the inhabitants of the world to choose their spiritual allegiance. Choose man and his materialism as your source, or God! This is God's way of pruning the world, separating the tares from the wheat and sifting the wheat for the final harvest. It is time for God to cut short the kingdom of men, for the millennium reign of Jesus is soon to come.

Clue #4   The Head Wound

The scriptures say, "I saw one of his heads as if it had

been mortally wounded, and his deadly wound was healed. And the world marveled and followed the beast." (Revelation 13:3) It's almost as if the Anti-Christ were raised from the dead! The world will perceive this as some sort of divine approval of the man's life, and will be inspired by the near fatal event to embrace his world viewpoints.

However, let's not rule out the possibility that this is purely allegorical. That the beast represents a figure of Nebuchadnezzar's Babylon of old, which was left for dead as a kingdom and power. Now low and behold, Mystery Babylon has risen from a deadly wound and is alive and well, ready to take dominion over the world again, in spirit instead of geographically, as Nebuchadnezzar did in the Old Testament.

Clue #5 Signs and Wonders

The Hollywood productions of today's action thrillers are packed with special effects. Although the silver screen is based upon imagination, there is a subtle influence upon the heart that somehow interprets its images to be based in authenticity. Often a crime is performed by duplicating the plot of a movie. Or a teenager drives his SUV with such reckless abandon, one wonders what influence he could have been under as he left the latest James Bond flick. Young, impressionable minds long for the capability to have such power over the natural world.

When the beast calls down fire from the heavens in the sight of men, mankind will accept this as some sort of divine validation of the Anti-Christ (Revelation 13:13). Amazingly, the beast even gives breath to the image of the Anti-Christ, so that it comes to life and speaks convincing words to the populace to worship the beast and his image (Revelation 13:15).

"The coming of the lawless one is according to the working of Satan, with all power, signs, and lying wonders...." (2 Thessalonians 2:9). Unlike David Copperfield's magic, these signs will be the real deal. They will be a seductive complement to the Anti-Christ's arsenal of compelling the nations to join his revolution. God forewarned the Israelites of Moses' day, of men who would be able to perform signs and wonders, with the motive of leading them astray to other gods. Certainly, Pharaoh's magicians were able to duplicate the miracle of Moses with their staffs becoming snakes as well. God said, "You must not listen to the words of that prophet...The Lord your **God is testing you** to find out whether you love him with all your heart and with all your soul" (Deuteronomy 13:1-3). Since it is clear that the powers are granted, one can only surmise that God is allowing Satan these abilities to fulfill God's will.

Those who are prone to seek after miracles and the paranormal will be extremely vulnerable to Satan's deceptions. Jesus declared, "For false christs [anointings] and false prophets will arise and show great signs and wonders, so as to deceive, if possible, even the elect" (Matthew 24:24). Christians who understand the truth of God's Word, will be prepared to overlook these awesome displays of power and recognize them for what they are, designed deceptions to entice pleasure seekers.

Clue #6 Worship of The Image

Like Nebuchadnezzar of ancient Babylon, the Anti-Christ of Mystery Babylon will require all to worship the image of the beast. Only time will tell exactly what this image ends up being. It may be an emblem, or statue, or a hologram, who knows? John the revelator tells us the image is given breath and the ability to speak and all that refuse to worship the image will be put to death (Revelation 13:15). It is also given the additional power to cause all to receive a mark, in order to buy and sell.

Nebuchadnezzar required all to worship his golden image and to consider it a privilege to be a part of his awesome empire. Likewise, the Anti-Christ will pressure all to respond with worship towards his image for the concession of participating in the utopian marketplace. Similarly, the Caesars of the Roman Empire required all to burn a pinch of incense unto their image as a god, in all public places.

Jesus perceived the wickedness of man, when they asked him if Jews should pay taxes to the Roman Empire. Jesus lifted up a coin and asked, "Whose image and superscription is this?" They responded, "Caesar's." Jesus wisely instructed them to "Render to Caesar, that which is Caesar's and to God, that which is God's" (Matthew 22:15-21).

The Anti-Christ's desire is to have total control in your life. When the Anti-Christ attaches worship to his economic system and thereby asks you to acknowledge him as your source of sustenance, each Christian will have to determine if worship belongs to Caesar or God. It may be a great market economy, but the Anti-Christ is not my source, God is! God is the only one who will receive my praise. It is entirely possible that worship will be a minimal discussion, that taking the mark is sufficient to declare your allegiance to the Anti-Christ as your source of sustenance. Whatever, true Christians will be wise enough to never allow a mark to be placed in their right hand or forehead for any purpose connected to buying, selling, or worship.

No one ever dreamed that a cult leader named Jim Jones could convince over nine hundred people to drink strychnine spiked cool-aid, leading them to their deaths. Each succeeding mass death leaves society bewildered as to how anyone could fall prey to the charms of a cult leader, who would betray them to death. The answer is simple; they did not read or believe the Bible. Instead, they listened to a flattering leader pontificate his utopian ideas until they themselves were persuaded. The Anti-Christ is the consummate cult leader, who convinces an unsuspecting world to follow his dreams. The world will not understand that destruction, spiritual death and the judgment of God will come upon all who take his mark.

Clue #7   The Strong Delusion

The Anti-Christ is revealed during a time called the "mystery of iniquity" (2 Thessalonians 2:1-12). Iniquity simply means lawlessness. The Holy Spirit has been holding back the spirit of lawlessness until the fullness of God's timetable. God's Ten Commandments are being violated today like never before. Our own post-Christian nation no longer has the spiritual fortitude to cleave to them. Instead, judges rule they must be taken down in our public schools. Consequently, violence is rampant and policemen with metal detectors patrol our public schools.

The title Anti-Christ simply means anti-messiah or unbelief that God has the power to save! Man simply does not feel a need to be saved. Mystery Babylon is the culmination of man's departure from trusting in God, to trusting in themselves, evidenced by the neglect of all the commandments, but especially the tenth, "You shall not covet" (Exodus 20:17). It is in this wicked climate, the enemy reveals himself "According to the working of Satan with all power, signs and lying wonders, and with all unrighteous deception...." *But the reason, the Anti-Christ is believed and received by all who perish, has more to do with God than Satan.* "For this reason **God will send** them strong delusion, that they should believe a lie, that they all may be condemned who did not believe the truth but had pleasure in unrighteousness" (2 Thessalonians 2:9-12).

Their sin and error is seeking first the kingdom of unrighteous pleasure. Because "They did not like to retain God in their knowledge, God gave them over to a debased mind, to do those things which are not fitting" (Romans 1:28). Man did not worship God the creator, so God gave him over to worship the creature and evolution. Man as the bride of Christ, did not worship God the bridegroom, so God gave him over to homosexuality and sexual perversion. Furthermore, man will not worship God as his savior-provider, so God will give him over to believe the beast-destroyer, "That no one might buy or sell except one who has the mark" (Revelation 13:17). People who are deluded think they are right, as do Darwinians and homosexuals, but they are in error. This kind of spiritual hardness frees Satan to manipulate the masses and bring them to destruction.

Remember the scriptures say, "If any one worships the beast and his image, and receives his mark on his forehead or on his hand, he himself shall ...be tormented with fire and brimstone in the presence of the holy angels and in the presence of the Lamb. And the smoke of their torment ascends forever and ever; and they have no rest day or night, who worship the beast and his image, and whoever receives the mark...." (Revelation 14:9-11).

Clue #8   Follow The Money, I Mean The Mark

The object of Satan's diabolical plan is not the money; it is the possession of your soul and ultimate allegiance through the spirit of covetousness. Access via the mark, to the money is merely the bait of covetousness as pornography is to sexual lust. A successful investigation of criminal activity usually invokes the old adage, follow the money. The same is true in grasping the Anti-Christ's economic system. By following the trail of covetousness, we can uncover the beast's scheme, about which the Apostle Paul warned Timothy.

"But those who **desire to be rich** fall into temptation and a snare, and into many foolish and harmful lusts which drown men in **destruction and perdition**. For **the love of money is the root of all evil,** for which some have strayed from the faith in their greediness, and pierced themselves through with many sorrows" (1Timothy 6:9-10). Like the fatal Venus fly trap, men follow wealth to their own spiritual destruction. There is a snare, a trap. You can't see it, but it is there for the purpose of taking you captive. Its beautiful, but fatal.

Now contrast Paul's admonitions to faithful Christians, "But you O man of God, **flee these things** [*the love of money*] and pursue righteousness, faith, love, patience, gentleness. **Fight the good fight of faith, lay hold of eternal life**...I urge you in the sight of God who gives life to all things, before Jesus Christ...keep this commandment without spot, blameless **until our Lord's appearing**...."   (1Timothy 6:11-14). Obviously before the return of Jesus Christ, Christians will be in a great struggle for eternal life which will require our fleeing the temptation of wealth.

Jesus said, "No man can serve two masters; for either

he will hate the one and love the other, or else he will be loyal to the one and despise the other. You cannot serve God and mammon" (Matthew 6:24). This fundamental spiritual truth will be clearly exposed in every man's life when he decides to accept or reject the mark. Like singles who check the ring for the availability of a prospective date, a glance of the hand or forehead will reveal every man's spiritual heart, for "Where your treasure is, there will be your heart also" (Matthew 6:21).

Three Angels of Judgment

In Revelation, three angels appear in heaven and urge the faithful to worship. The first angel proclaims the hour of God's judgment has come, therefore worship the creator who is our source. The second angel declares, "Babylon is fallen.... because she made all nations drink of the wine of the wrath of her fornication." The third angel shouts the judgment of hell for anyone taking the mark of the beast, and attaches, "Here is the patience of the saints; here are those who keep the commandments of God and the faith of Jesus" (Revelation 14:6-12). Alas, God's hour of judgment simply means the evidence has all been presented and the judge is now ready to give the verdict. God uses this end-time scheme of Satan to separate out those who are appointed for destruction, who chose the mark so they could continue their covetous lifestyle. And ordain to eternal life, those who decided to trust the Lord during these extremely difficult days, even if it means the loss of their life (v13).

I once heard the story of a wise man that supposedly could answer anyone's question. So a mischievous boy caught a butterfly, and clasped it in his hands as he approached the elderly sage. The confident youth challenged, "The butterfly in my palm, is it dead or alive?" The prudent voice never wavered as he firmly replied, "If I say to you it is alive, you will instantly squeeze it and present it to me dead. And if I say to you he is dead, you will open your hands and let it fly away. Therefore, within your hand you hold the power of life and death!" During this season of the world's testing, people will possess within their hand the power to choose eternal life or eternal death, by accepting or rejecting the mark.

The Pharisees once asked Jesus when the coming of the kingdom would be. Jesus responded by saying, "The kingdom of God does not come with observation; nor will they say, 'See here!' or 'See there!' For indeed, the kingdom of God is within you" (Luke 17:20). Jesus is saying to them who are anxious about all these things, calm down, resolve yourselves to love the Lord with all your heart. To allow God's strength and character help you make the right choice in that day and hour. For you hold within yourselves the gift of free will, to choose God on a daily basis and thereby eternal life.

I am not a robot. No one commands me to love, that is my choice. A love relationship is the unrivaled intimacy between two individuals who choose to build one another up for a lifetime. Even God by His volition does not make me worship Him. Neither the Anti-Christ, Satan, nor anyone else can make me worship them. It is a decision on my part. It is the greatest gift of God, free will. It is what makes man unique in all of God's creation. From the Garden of Eden until Christ's return, there is a war going on for our allegiance. I will not be "deceived by any means." I choose to love and worship God!

Chapter 7

Mystery Babylon's Fiery Furnace
"The Persecution of the Church"

*"And he shall speak great words against the most High,
and shall wear out the saints of the most High..."*
Daniel 7:25

Jesus instructed each of His disciples, "Come and Follow me." In the process of following Jesus, I am keenly aware of two reasons why He was crucified. The first reason is that His enemies said Jesus forbade the paying of tribute to Caesar. The second reason is that Jesus claimed to be the Son of God (Luke 22:70-71 23:2). The same two charges will be leveled against those who reject the mark of the Anti-Christ.

In similar fashion, the Chaldeans (Babylonians) of Nebuchadnezzar's kingdom accused the righteous Jews, Shadrach, Meshach and Abednego. They said of them, "These men, O king have not regarded you...nor worshipped the golden image which you set up" (Daniel 3:12). Their reason for not bowing down of course, they were sons of the Most High God. Their sin was refusing to worship, and their punishment was the fiery furnace.

Moreover, Daniel was put in the lion's den for refusing to pray exclusively to King Darius. It was because of Daniel's devotion to God that they found occasion to accuse (Daniel 6:5). The disciples of Jesus in like manner each suffered martyrdom. Legend has it that Peter begged to be crucified upside down, considering himself unworthy to be crucified as Jesus was. The Apostle John was more fortunate. Tradition records he was only boiled in oil for his refusal to worship Caesar as

God.   Like the apostles, many who live in the last generation will be martyred for refusing to worship the image of the Anti-Christ (Revelation 20:4). What is their sin? Refusing to worship the image of the beast, because they are the sons of God.

As Jesus was being led away to the crucifixion, several women mourned and lamented the Lord. Jesus said something that sends chills up my spine, "Do not weep for Me, weep for yourselves and your children. For indeed the days are coming...they will begin 'to say to the mountains, "Fall on us!" and to the hills, "Cover us!"'" for if they do these things in the green wood, what will be done in the dry?" (Luke 23:28-31). The phrase regarding the mountains, "Fall on us and cover us!" is emphatic of the judgement Day of Jesus Christ (Isaiah 2:10-11+17-21 Revelation 6:14-17). Just prior to His return will be the greatest holocaust ever recorded in history.

Tyrants Who Massacre

One imagines how can ruthless political leaders be so murderous?   On a recent visit to Central Asia, I encountered a people who were formally of the Soviet Union, but now had broken away to restore their former nation of Karalkalpakstan.   When I inquired of their national hero, I was shown a statue of "Emur Temur" that had replaced the statue of Stalin in the Town Square. Who is he and what is his claim to fame? He was the great grandson of Genghis Khan.   Apparently, he conquered more geography in Central Asia than anyone in the history of the nationals. He did it by massacring his opposition and supposedly killed so many people, that his own leaders told him to back off or there wouldn't be anyone left to rule.

"Why would you revere a guy like that," I inquired? "Because we Asians are not like you Americans. We don't want to debate the issues; we want a strong leader who will lead and govern with an iron fist. The people respect this kind of leadership that controls the masses," replied my native guide. Suddenly it dawned on me, it doesn't really matter what is right and wrong, or whether it agrees with my American upbringing, there are cultures who embrace this totalitarian "kill them if you have to" style of government.   So much for Stalin, apparently he demonstrated weakness in killing only a few hundred thousand.

Suddenly the likes of Saddam Hussein made perfect sense from the cultural perspective. Here is a killer who used chemical warfare against the Kurds of his own land. Their sin was being less than genetically pure as an Arab. Saddam ingratiates himself to the Arab world by aspiring to destroy Israel, thus gaining allegiance with the radical nationalistic spirit of the Arab countries. The sentiment of the countrymen is one of adoration for a strong leader who will stop at nothing.

Recently at our annual Pastors' conference, it was announced that a missionary from Africa had been spared of his life because the ministerial leadership had given helped him catch a flight out of his warring homeland of Sierra Leone. To my astonishment, he was seated at the table eating dinner with me. He began to explain that a coup had been planned and the militia leaders were dropping by to ask him to pray for God's blessings on their rebellion.   When he refused, saying that God required him to pray "for kings, and all in authority" according to 1 Timothy 2:2, they told him he would be executed for his lack of loyalty to them. With my mouth full of tasty German Chocolate cake, he briskly dropped several pictures in front of my plate. There were the dismembered bodies of his loved ones, stacked in front of his church. I gagged in horror!

Our sheltered American democracy can not grasp the tyrannical brutality that exists in foreign cultures. Whether it is the massacre of Serbs and Croations in former Yugoslavia or the Rwandan tribes of Africa, Cambodia's Pol Pot, or Vietnam's K'mer Rouge, villains who kill to acquire power will be very much a part of the twenty first century mindset.

Spoils and Plundering

Mystery Babylon's persecution of Christians will begin with an ancient strategy. It was always typical of Old Testament kings to spoil their enemy after defeating him on the battlefield. Their possessions were looted to undermine the adversary's ability to recover strength, while fortifying the kingdom of the victor. These spoils were often given to the people of the kingdom as gifts celebrating the victory. They were also used to ingratiate the people to the victorious king (1 Samuel 30:21-31).

Likewise, the Anti-Christ is going to confiscate the possessions of Christians and redistribute the wealth. The Prophet Daniel records, "The robbers of your people shall exalt themselves to establish the vision...he shall scatter among them the prey, and spoil, and riches." He goes on to say of the Anti-Christ, "He shall return into his land with great riches; and his heart shall be against the holy covenant...they that understand among the people shall instruct many: yet they shall fall by the sword, and by flame, by captivity, and by spoil many days...he ...shall divide the land for gain" (Daniel 11:14+24+28+33+39). The Anti-Christ will "Have accomplished to scatter the power of the holy people...." (Daniel 12:7). The Hebrew rendering of the word "power" means wealth.

The Apostle Paul recorded the same principle of being spoiled by the Roman Empire. "But recall the former days in which, after you were illuminated, you endured a great struggle with sufferings: ...while you were made a spectacle both by reproaches and tribulation, and partly while you became companions of those who were so treated; for you had compassion on me in my chains, and joyfully accepted the plundering of your goods, knowing that you have a better and an enduring possession for yourselves in heaven" (Hebrews 10:32-34). Wow! Just as Solomon said, there is nothing new under the sun. What will happen to Christians during this persecution by the Anti-Christ took place in ancient Babylon under Nebuchadnezzar (Daniel 1:1-2). Moreover, it happened to Paul and the first church during their persecutions under Caesar of the Roman Empire.

Now listen to how Paul finishes his thought about this plundering of your goods; "Therefore do not cast away your confidence, which has a great reward. For you have need of endurance, so that after you have done the will of God, you may receive the promise: For yet a little while, and He who is coming will come and will not tarry. Now the just shall live by faith; but if anyone draws back, My soul shall have no pleasure in him. But we are not of those who draw back to perdition, but of those who believe to the saving of the soul" (Hebrews 10:35-39). This passage describes precisely the tribulation of enduring the Anti-Christ's wicked persecution; the same as the saints had to endure during the Roman Empire. His admonishment is to have patience, because Jesus will come and reward you for not taking the mark of the beast, and caving in to his persecution.

The Clout of the Free Lunch

I once heard a story about the power of a free lunch, which illustrates the Anti-Christ's strategy to take God's people captive. The story goes that a wild boar lived in the woods, near a community of people. It was well known that the wild boar could out fox any hunter. One day a new hunter arrived and announced he was going to capture the wild boar without firing a shot. The community laughed him to scorn. Undaunted, he took his wagon out to the deepest part of the woods and laid out several wooden planks on the ground, with some grain on top. Of course, the wild boar came to investigate, but refused the offering because of the unfamiliar boards. However, as the weeks passed by and the hunter never returned, the wild boar decided to nibble at the grain. Enjoying the free lunch, he devoured it and headed back to the underbrush. When the hunter returned some weeks later, he rejoiced, "I got you now, your mine, all mine!" The hunter repeated the process, this time digging a hole and covering it with the planks and replacing the grain. Once again the wild boar came to investigate, but refused because of the fragrance of the fresh dirt. As the weeks passed and the hunter did not return, the wild boar finally gave in and returned for the grain. Again, the hunter marveled, "Your mine, all mine!" Each time the hunter would repeat the process, removing a board on each visit until finally the wild boar was so accustomed to the free lunch, he stepped out onto the boards for the grain, only to discover they were all missing and fell into the hole. The mighty hunter tied up the wild boar and returned to the community, who marveled, "How did you capture that wild boar?" It was easy replied the wise old hunter,

"It was the clout of the free lunch!" The Anti-Christ will use the power of the free lunch to continue his ambition of bringing everyone under his captivity.

Jesus foretold the events of the last days this way, "You will be betrayed even by parents and brothers and relatives and friends; and they will send some of you to your death. And you will be hated by all for My name's sake. But not a hair of your head shall be lost. In your patience, possess your souls" (Luke 21:16-19). Blood is thicker than water, what could possibly come between the closest of relatives ...unless it is money? Family inheritances and the dividing of wealth will rip apart family strongholds in a heartbeat. The American Indians are a prime example. They fought long and hard to get federal recognition of their tribal ancestries. Now many of them are warring amongst themselves over control of their casinos!

Is it possible the Anti-Christ will offer incentives to the masses to report rebellious Christians? After all, if you don't have a mark you are not on the books, and these traitors must be rooted out of the world system, or they will hinder its effectiveness. Families know the confession of other family members perfectly. Daniel said, "He shall have intelligence with them that forsake the holy covenant...such as do wickedly against the covenant shall he corrupt with flatteries...." (Daniel 11:30+32). In this scenario, it makes perfect sense how the family could come unglued, to the point of putting each other to death, especially if it meant you were going to gain the family fortunes as a reward for your loyalty to the Anti-Christ. Many will justify themselves with thoughts of patriotism as they dispassionately betray their Christian kin to satisfy their covetous spirit. Like a junkie who plunders the house of his parents in order to get drug money, it will be the same with the Anti-Christ's strategy of spoiling the enemy. "Because lawlessness will abound the love of many will grow cold" (Matthew 24:10). This way the Anti-Christ will continue to take captives and establish his strong hold on the earthly kingdom. It will be said of him, "Who is like unto the beast? Who is able to make war with him?" (Revelations 13:4). Fortunately, the scriptures say that despite of all his wickedness, he cannot "touch a hair of my head" (Luke 21:18), meaning my soul.

This is ruthless! How could anyone be so vicious? The answer lies in the lust of Satan for power and as the ruler of this world system; he will go to great lengths to secure his kingdom. Revelation declares, "For the devil has come down to you, having great wrath, because he knows that he has a short time" (Revelation 12:12). As the father of lies, he even deceives himself into believing he can somehow pull this off and conquer God. "And I saw the beast, and the kings of the earth, and their armies, gather together to make war against Him who sat on the horse and against His army" (Revelation 19:19).

No wonder Jesus said, "In your patience you possess your souls." This kind of terrorism will stretch the seams of the strongest faith when one sees the hedonism displayed; it will make your blood boil. Each Christian will be tempted to take matters into his own hands and exact justice. But Jesus warned, "He who kills with the sword must be killed with the sword. Here is the patience and faith of the saints" (Revelation 13:10). Christians will have to learn to be wise as serpents and harmless as doves in order to survive.

How Long, O Lord?

In ancient Babylon, Nebuchaddnezzar sentenced Shadrach, Meshach and Abednego to the fiery furnace, for refusing to worship the golden image. Repeatedly Daniel warns of the future Anti-Christ's hatred for the saints. "He made war with the saints and prevailed against them; Until the Ancient of Days came" (Daniel 7:21-22). And the same thought is mirrored in Mystery Babylon, "And it was granted to him [Anti-Christ] to make war with the saints and to overcome them..." (Revelation 13:7). This season of persecution will indeed test the patience of the saints, as we cry out to God for His intervention.

Again Daniel says, "They shall fall by the sword...And some of them of the understanding shall fall, to try them, and to purge them, and make them white, even to the time of the end...." (Daniel 11:33+35). As in ancient Babylon, similarly, Mystery Babylon is indicted by the Holy Spirit, "In her was found the blood of the prophets and saints, and of all who were slain on the earth" (Revelation 18:24).

In the Old Testament, just as a new king would kill the offspring of the former king in order to secure the kingdom from any rivals, the Anti-Christ correspondingly kills the saints, children of the King of Kings. "And I saw the souls of those who had been beheaded for their witness of Jesus and for the word of God, who had not worshipped the beast or his image, and had not received his mark on their foreheads or on their hands" (Revelation 20:4). It is understandable in this context, why the saints cry out, "How long, O Lord, holy and true, until You judge and avenge our blood on those who dwell on the earth?" (Revelation 6:10). The Apostle Paul said,

"We must through many tribulations enter the kingdom of God" (Acts 14:22). This will not be a time to make war against the Anti-Christ, but instead to endure with faith and patience as we trust our heavenly Father.

Hitler's Shadow

Older men of God have taught a principle that has served me well in discerning truth. Their principle is based on a scripture, "First in the natural, then the spiritual" (1 Corinthians 15:46).   With this thought in mind, could it be that God was giving the church a visual aid to discern the future, with the historical event of Hitler's Nazi Germany and his massacre of the Jews?

Here was a civil country that was so enamored with the charm and political savvy of an up and coming leader named Hitler, that they gave themselves to follow him in the greatest atrocities known to man. They started out simply trying to jump-start their economy. However, as the economy began to revive, they found themselves fueling their national patriotism with war, by defeating and spoiling the neighboring countries and their domestic Jews.   Then their leader began to promote the final solution, which was purifying the race by eliminating the Jews in Nazi "SS" concentration camps. The Jews were spoiled of their possessions, being forced to sign over their personal fortunes, businesses and valuables. Then they were hauled off in cattle cars to the gas chambers. Over six million Jews were killed before the sympathy of the western world was awakened to their demise and liberated them. The world was horrified at the inhumane treatment of the Jews. Germany surrendered in May of 1945. Three years later in May of 1948, Israel was born as a nation.

Consider the parallels of Nazi Germany to ancient Babylon and Revelation's Mystery Babylon. All three have dictators who take God's people captive, spoil their wealth, and begin to kill them. The sympathy of a superior power is evoked and a rescue is made, freeing them to come to their own kingdom.

I believe God is trying to tell Christians something. The memories of Nazi Germany are still vivid as we hear of Jewish families who are still trying to recover their families' possessions from European countries. The Nation of Israel cries, "never again!" But it will happen in the spiritual, just as it has happened in the natural.

Christians, the true children of God, will be maligned by a clever politician on the rise, who will convince the world their annihilation is the solution to purifying mankind to world utopia. They will be spoiled because they refuse to take the mark and then systematically killed, evoking the sympathy of our God, who sends our Lord Jesus Christ to gather us, to give us our place with him during His millennial reign.

Secular college professors are already planting the seeds of this future scenario. The evidence is shown by their disciples who proclaim, "the problem with the world today is religion." These students echo the classroom sentiment that all the wars of history are because of man's pursuit of ethnic religions. These students will be our future leaders who will insist on religion being subordinate to the world system of following the Anti-Christ as God and participation in the world marketplace by taking the mark.

Belshazzar's Mistake

In ancient Babylon, Nebuchadnezzar discovered the

revealing of the Son of Man when he persecuted the three Hebrew children (Daniel 3:25). Belshazzar discovered the handwriting on the wall when he mocked God with the vessels of the Jerusalem temple (Daniel 5:3-5). Paul said to the saints, "Do you not know that your body is the temple of the Holy Spirit...whom you have from God, and you are not your own?" (1 Corinthians 6:19). Concerning the knowledge of our salvation, Paul further stated, "We have this treasure in earthen vessels, that the excellence of the power may be of God and not of us" (2 Corinthians 4:7).

When the Anti-Christ abuses the saints who are the true vessels of the heavenly Jerusalem by making a mockery of them in the persecution, the handwriting will be on the wall. The scriptures declare, "Babylon the great is fallen, is fallen...in one hour your judgment is come...rejoice over her, O heaven, and you holy apostles and prophets, for God has avenged you on her!" (Revelation 18:2+9+20). In an instant, the men of the earth will be crying out to the mountains and rocks, "Fall on us, and hide us from the face of him that sits on the throne, and the wrath of the Lamb: For the great day of his wrath is come and who shall be able to stand?" (Revelation 6:14-17). What a glorious moment it will be for the faithful saints of God who endured until the end.

Chapter 8

Mystery Babylon's Shadrach, Meshach and Abednego!
"The Great Revival"

"The harvest is the end of the age!" Matthew 13:39

When Nebuchadnezzar confronted Shadrach, Meshach and Abednego over their refusal to worship the golden image, several dynamics were at work. The king demanded total submission, even in spiritual reverence. The Hebrew children refused to worship because the first and second commandments had been ingrained in them from their youth. They were not to have any gods before the Lord God and they were not to worship any graven images. Of course, the infuriated king persecuted them by having them thrown into the fiery furnace. His persecution of them resulted in the revealing of the fourth man in the fiery furnace, the Son of God.

The character and purity of heart exemplified by the three Hebrew children resulted in an interesting proclamation by the repentant Nebuchadnezzar. "Blessed be the God of Shadrach, Meshach and Abednego, who...delivered his servants that trusted in him, and have changed the King's word, and yielded their bodies, that they might not serve nor worship any god, except their own God. Therefore I make a decree, that every people, nation, and language, which speak anything amiss against the God of Shadrach, Meshach, and Abednego, shall be cut in pieces, and their houses shall be made a dunghill: because there is no other God that can deliver after this sort" (Daniel 3:28-30).

The Anti-Christ of Mystery Babylon will not make

any such proclamations: however, because the church is willing to suffer the persecution of the beast with faith and patience, the net result will be the same.   When mankind sees the integrity of God's people, unwilling to bow before the image of the beast and refusing to take the mark, they will discern that Christians are in essence changing the Anti-Christ's word.   He said all must worship and people will not be able to survive without the mark. Both of which are nullified by the loyalty of Christians to Jesus Christ. Through this endurance of suffering persecution and yielding even their bodies to be martyred, the world will come to know the God of Christianity.

The reflection of the church, "without spot or blemish" will have a powerful influence on the hearts of the world, bringing them to the greatest revival man has ever known!   The disciples asked Jesus for an explanation of the parable of the tares of the field. Jesus said, "The field is the world, the good seeds are the sons of the kingdom, but the tares are the sons of the wicked one...the harvest is the end of the age!"   (Matthew 13:36-39).   Did you get that?   "The harvest is the end of the age!"   As we see the wickedness of these last days wax worse and worse, the Apostle Paul tells us where "Sin abounds, grace will much more abound"   (Romans 5:20). In addition, many will be persuaded to refuse the covetous lifestyle of Mystery Babylon and instead follow Jesus Christ.

The Revival of 1948

One of the greatest revivals of the last century was generated in 1948, when Israel became a nation. The sparks of that historic moment ignited the resurgent flames of evangelism all over America. Older men of

God reminisce of 200 plus traveling tent crusades that canvassed America preaching the born again message. A couple of those early tent revivalists are Reverend Oral Roberts and Evangelist Billy Graham. And America was ready to respond. The 1950's saw thousands pour down the sawdust aisles to receive Christ as their Savior. The sixties gave way to the Jesus movement, as the children of war veterans called hippies searched for love and peace and found it in the arms of Jesus Christ. The political turmoil of the seventies gave way to the charismatic renewal, as Christians began to experience the power of the Holy Spirit. The revival continued in the eighties as Christians embraced the faith movement.

The preparation of America for that revival was accomplished in the decades prior to Israel becoming a nation in 1948. My grandfather, who was born in the 1890's, used to tell me of the zealous preaching of faithful men. He said their message in the early decades of the 1900's was, the prophets have foretold, and the day is coming when Israel will become a nation again in their homeland of Palestine. He told me they were ridiculed to scorn by men who would scoff at the notion. After all, Israel had been scattered to the Four Corners of the earth for the last two millenniums.

My grandfather reflected on a common phrase of his peers. Just as today when people say, "The chance of this or that happening is a snow ball's chance in hell," people would say back then, "I'll believe it when Israel becomes a nation again in Palestine." In other words, there was tremendous doubt and unbelief concerning the prophetic word of God.

Like the persistent striking of a flint stone, patiently waiting for the right spark to catch fire, these Godly men kept standing on the prophetic Word of God anticipating the fulfillment of His promise. They endured the mocking of carnal men, ignored their blinded hearts and faithfully preached the signs of the times. For decades, men laughed and scoffed until suddenly, in a time of war and international confusion, Israel emerged as a nation! Like homing pigeons drawn to their perch, the seeds of God's Word began to germinate in the hearts of men as they realized the truth of God's salvation message. The obvious fulfillment of prophecy was recognized because courageous preachers forged ahead with God's truth, preparing men's hearts with the knowledge of the Biblical promise. Revival resulted from the emergence of Israel's national existence, which continued forty years.

Revival Repeat

As we enter the twenty-first century, our work is cut out for us, just as it was in my grandfather's time. During the covetous nineties, the revival stalled and church growth leveled off. At a recent church seminar, the leaders acknowledged most churches that are growing are doing so primarily from transfer growth. The seminar leaders then proceeded to teach pastors how to draw a crowd with upscale technology. Frankly, I am not interested in putting on a spiritual floorshow, nor am I interested in growth for number's sake. God cannot be pleased with this poor substitution of trying to compete with the world. Unless people build their convictions on the Word of God, they will be shallow and ready to fall at the tremors of persecution. Instead, we must begin to prepare men's hearts with the realities of God's Word concerning the revealing of the Anti-Christ, his persecution of the church and the revelation of Jesus Christ!

I perceive in the coming years, men will confront Christians with skepticism because Jesus did not return as the saints were expecting at the turn of the millennium. Peter says, "Scoffers will come in the last days...saying, 'where is the promise of His coming?'" (2 Peter 3:3-4). Consequently, they will criticize the church and give themselves to pursuing worldly lusts with abandonment, ignoring Christians for the most part and writing us off as irrelevant. It will be time for the church to come out of it's own disillusionment and begin to see God's will and purpose for this last generation. That Christians have been called to arise and prepare the world for the greatest revival known to man.

The next great event on the prophetic calendar is, "Concerning the coming of the Lord Jesus Christ and our gathering together to Him, we ask you, not to be soon shaken in mind or troubled...**for that Day will not come unless...the man of sin is revealed, the son of perdition**" (2 Thessalonians 2:1-3). The preparation of men's hearts will require the fortitude of courageous preachers who will sow the seeds of truth. No doubt, we will be mocked and ridiculed as my grandfather's generation was and as the Prophet Jeremiah. His own people cast the righteous prophet into a pit, where he sank in the mire. Nevertheless, the seeds of revival require the plowing of hardened hearts. This persecution is part of the price that must be paid in order to see genuine repentance. Their mocking serves to make men question the truth, to seek for answers and to ponder the Word of God for wisdom.

As Mystery Babylon's spirit of covetousness continues to rob society of it's spiritual life and as future events reveal the emergence of the Anti-Christ, there will be a spiritual awakening much like that of 1948, only greater. The revival will be fueled by the world's observance of faithful Christians being persecuted, but enduring with patience. The Roman Empire fueled the revival of the early church with its unjust treatment of righteous Christians who refused to honor Caesar as a god. Likewise, many will see the Godly character of end time saints and be drawn to the truth. Decades of mocking the revealing of the Anti-Christ will give way to a landslide of people desiring to trust the Lord as their savior. For when men see the prophecy shaping into existence, evidenced by the mandating of the micro-chip's implantation, the next revival will be ignited. The clarity of the prophetic fulfillment will germinate the seeds of God's Word concerning these last days. Multitudes will be asking the same question they did of Peter on the day of Pentecost, "Men and brethren, what shall we do?" The answer will be the same, "Repent and be baptized in the name of Jesus Christ for the remission of sins" (Acts 2:37-38).   As the Anti-Christ is revealed and the persecution of the saints intensifies, so the desire of spiritually hungry men wanting to join the just cause of living for Jesus Christ will intensify.   In this next generation, "The earth shall be full of the knowledge of the Lord, as the waters cover the sea" (Isaiah 11:9).

Understanding Persecution

A good friend who is a missionary, taught me the value of persecution. The nature of his ministry, preaching the gospel in the streets of London, evokes enormous consternation from the hard and proud British. He is regularly cussed, spit upon and even splattered with rotten eggs. He responds with outbursts of rejoicing and shouts of alleluia. He explained to me what Jesus said,

"Blessed are those who are persecuted for righteousness' sake, for theirs is the kingdom of heaven. Blessed are you when they revile and persecute you, and say all manner of evil against you falsely for my sake. Rejoice and be exceedingly glad, for great is your reward in heaven, for so they persecuted the prophets who were before you" (Matthew 5:10-12). For some reason, I had always interpreted people's negatives as though I was doing it wrong when sharing the good news. Now I have learned the negatives are a fair indication that people resent your decision to live for Jesus and their anger reveals the condition of their carnal heart.

We regularly preach in the open air on the college campuses of our community, exercising our first amendment right, the freedom of speech. Our ministry team has covenanted together to keep our message centered on the good news of the gift of salvation and to avoid the spirit of condemnation, preferring to allow the Holy Spirit to work in man's heart the conviction of sin. That way, when persecution comes we know it is man's carnality surfacing. After all, who could be upset with the knowledge that Jesus died for their sins and offers the gift of eternal life? That is GOOD NEWS. Unless of course, their self-centered, proud, carnal hearts refuse to allow them to believe they need a savior. The result is often times students mock, cuss, repudiate, chuck us with pennies and paper balls, turn our tracts into paper airplanes, burn our tracts with their lighters, threaten us with physical harm and many times call the police, who in turn try to intimidate us with handcuffs and arrest. We, of course, respond visibly with rejoicing and gladness, so they know we are totally confident of our convictions, just as Shadrach, Meshach and Abednego were.

People frequently tell us that no one is listening and we

are wasting our time. But the truth is the persecution develops our spiritual muscles of faith and patience, enabling us to endure greater trials. Plus, many see the unjust treatment and are moved to support us with their encouragement. Finally, some receive Christ at the end of a public sermon, while many return to speak with us later to tell us they have been thinking about what we preach and desire to receive salvation. Alleluia! Rejoice and be exceedingly glad!

The Roman persecution fueled the growth of the first century church. Mystery Babylon will do the same for the church in the last days. Just as rain is needed for our crops to grow and our wells to replenish, so persecution works to nourish and strengthen the church. How? The same way rain forms, from the clash of warm and cold air masses. The turbulence of opposing forces results in the sweet moisture of heaven falling to cause everything to grow. The harvest follows this process in both the natural and spiritual realm.

The persecution we experience on a weekly basis in our evangelism outreaches is the same that Christians will endure in the coming decades. As Christians learn the value of dealing with persecution and standing up for their conviction, in the face of a degenerate world who is embracing Mystery Babylon's utopian dreams, they will experience all of the spiritual benefits mentioned above.

One Hundred and Forty Four Thousand

A Jehovah witness once tried to convince me to join his church. I asked him how many people were going to get into paradise and he told me "One hundred and forty four thousand." I promptly asked him how many people were in the Jehovah witnesses worldwide? He replied five million. "Why should I join, I wouldn't have much chance of being one of the one hundred and forty four thousand," was my retort!

Interesting perceptions are given about the 144,000 of Revelation Chapter 7. One group suggests these are the virtuous Jewish saints who are left behind after the rapture, who preach the gospel and lead worldwide revival. Strangely, in Revelation 14 they reappear with Christ on Mount Zion with no conversions.

There is a reasonable explanation of this symbolic figure of the twelve tribes of Israel; for it is not a literal number.   The Anti-Christ is orchestrating what he believes is a utopian government. This Mystery Babylon is the culmination of man's wisdom, ingenuity and technology. It is also void of God.   In numerology, the number twelve is symbolic of perfect government. Therefore in the creating of a nation, God gave Jacob twelve sons that became the twelve tribes of Israel. The names of these twelve tribes will be on the twelve gates of the New Jerusalem, the dwelling place of God's saints in the future.   Jesus had twelve disciples.   They were the leaders God used to govern His people.

Whenever the number is multiplied, its intensity is an emphasis of its truth. The 144,000 are an emphasis of God's perfect government in contrast to the Anti-Christ utopian government. The Christians dwelling under the persecution of the Anti-Christ, who refuse the mark of the beast, are demonstrating the true government of God. The Anti-Christ believes men need to be controlled, but God's people are temperate, exercising self-control in all things. They don't panic over the thought of being shut out of the market place for refusing the mark. They, "Do not worry, saying 'what shall we eat?' or what shall we drink?' or 'what shall we wear?'" instead, they trust the living God who said, "Your heavenly Father knows that you need all these things" (Matthew 6:32-33).

A Christian, who allows Christ to be Lord, exemplifies the Wisdom of Solomon. "He who is slow to anger is better than the mighty and he who rules his spirit than he who takes a city" (Proverbs 16:32). The 144,000 is a reflection of God's lordship which is the true government, far better than anything man can offer. Listen to Solomon's observation, "Whoever has no rule over his own spirit, is like a city broken down, without walls" (Proverbs 25:28). This is a perfect description of those who follow the Anti-Christ in covetousness. Their spiritual walls are broken down and the enemy Satan, just walks right in and takes them captive at his will. But God's people are not so! Instead, they walk in perfect temperance in the most adverse conditions of persecution, exercising faith and patience as they wait upon God for guidance and comfort. What a contrast to the covetous weaklings who piously bow before the image of the beast and worship with disingenuous reverence, just to maintain their standard of living. This is not utopia...this is carnality!

In the Old Testament, when Israel was in proper spiritual relationship, God's people were governed only by the priests and judges. It was not until they rejected God and desired to be like the pagan nations, that God gave them a king (1 Samuel 8:4-9). When Christians walk in true relationship with God, they do not need to be governed by anyone but Jesus their High Priest.

Those who notice the confident poise of the Christian in this hour will long for the spiritual strength and character they have. It will only come with submission to Jesus Christ as Lord. For He is the true Kings of Kings and Lord of Lords, He is our perfect government.

Generation X...Extreme in Godliness!

Jesus said, "Lift up your eyes and look upon the fields, for they are white unto harvest" (John 4:35). A survey discovered two interesting truths about Generation X. First, 94% said they believe in God! Second, their foremost anxiety is financial security. This generation is primed and ready for whoever will promise them the future. Think about it, the Anti-Christ is going to declare himself to be God and if you want financial security, it will be achieved through taking the mark of the beast.

But correspondingly, these same youths have grown up with the best of everything materially. They wear $160.00 Air Jordan's, Tommy Hilfinger clothing, and drive Mustang convertibles to their senior high classes. At some point, they will come to a crossroads. That junction is a choice between the pursuit of a better standard of living than their parents had, which means even more greed and longer hours of exhausting work, to the demise of their personal health and family, or a simpler life. Many will see the true riches of Christians who illustrate the very life they long for. They will see people who understand the value of family, commitment to God and each other, who walk in peace and joy. Christians, who treasure something so deeply they are willing to die for God.

And this is precisely the pondering of their heart. Is there anything left in this world that one is willing to die for, something of true worth? These individuals have experienced the best the world has to offer, but they haven't experienced the Holy Spirit. The preaching of the last days is going to offer to the world the opportunity to know the one true God. The God who owns "the cattle on a thousand hills" and is more than able to meet our needs and give us eternal security. To this God we shall bow and worship, the God who refuses to be worshipped by any graven image, because "God is Spirit, and those who worship Him must worship Him in Spirit and in truth" (John 4:24).

Generation X is longing for the truth of that spirit, something they can really live for, something they can die for! Ironically, the universal personal identification code is abbreviated "UPIC." "You pick, you choose!" If Generation X is given the truth about these last days, ultimately they will make the right choice, they are burned out with meaningless materialism. They have discovered the harsh reality of Solomon's wisdom, "He who loves silver, **will never be satisfied** with silver, nor he who loves abundance with increase: this is also vanity" (Ecclesiastes 5:10). They have become a dry land in heart, like the children of Israel who wandered in the desert for forty years. God had given the Jews the desire of their lustful hearts, but with it came leanness of soul. Generation X has experienced the best the world can offer and yet their souls are on empty. They long for a cause and that cause is living and dying for Jesus Christ who said, "If any one thirsts, let him come to Me and drink. He who believes in Me", as the Scripture has said, "out of his heart will flow living water" (John 7:37-38). Generation X is going to choose to live for Christ and refuse the mark of the beast. They are the seeds of this last day revival.

"Les Miserabe" is a great movie that describes the spirit of Mystery Babylon. The movie brings home the value of loving God and your fellow man. It reveals the truth of those who pride themselves with money and self-righteousness, that they are "the miserable." The movie is worth viewing or reading the novel.

The Super Fry Deception

Mystery Babylon's lure of wealth is like buying fries at the fast food restaurant. I love fries. In fact, I can make a meal out of nothing but a super fry. But many times I have been frustrated as I pull away from the drive through window. As I open the bag and pull out the golden fries, I am dismayed at the quantity of crispy potatoes barely showing themselves above the lower front rim of the box. This discouraging scenario has occurred so many times, that now I go inside to get my fries. When the cashier brings my super fry, I immediately take them out of the bag and hold them up for all to see. Then I innocently proclaim, "All I want is for my fries to look like that advertisement, after all, a super fry should be super, like that picture on the plate glass window." The managerial embarrassment is immediately dealt with by refilling the box to over flowing. Now that is a super fry!

An employee later confessed to me, that management instructs them to short fill the boxes to increase the profits. Mystery Babylon does exactly the same. It advertises that life will be wonderful, filled to capacity if you will follow her seductiveness. But in reality, her real desire is to short fry your life, to rob you of your soul by luring your allegiance to the Anti-Christ. The manager's greed serves himself for profit, not the customer. Satan's real motive has more to do with ingratiating his ego with the loss of your opportunity for salvation, than serving any of your economic needs. Those who realize they are being short-fried by Mystery Babylon, will long for the fullness of life that only comes from serving Jesus Christ.

Haggai's Prophesy

The Prophet Haggai declares the revival of the last days. It is interesting to note the context of his admonitions. The Jews had previously returned to Jerusalem and their homeland from the captivity of Babylon. However, instead of rebuilding the foundation of the Lord's temple, they contented themselves with pursuing worldly possessions. Haggai the Prophet, seeing their laziness towards God's temple exhorts, "Is it time for you yourselves to dwell in your paneled houses, and this temple to lie in ruins?"...Consider your ways! You have sown much, and bring in little; you eat, but do not have enough; you drink, but you are not filled with drink; you clothe yourselves, but no one is warm; and he who earns wages, earns wages to put into a bag with holes. Thus says the Lord of hosts: "Consider your ways!" (Haggai 1:4-7).

As a Christian in the twenty-first century, does this sound like he is describing you? Are you constantly pursuing wealth, but feel you are spinning your wheels? If so read carefully, because he gives you the answer to your dilemma. The Jews' problem was they had left Babylon geographically, but were still in Babylon spiritually. They just carried it back with them to Jerusalem. They were really no better off for their return. They were still walking unrepentant of the very thing that had sent them to Babylon, seventy years before. They were not giving God's house first place in their lives. Oh God was there, but He was second priority in their lives. Is this the way it is for you? Is God's house second place to your personal pleasure of sleep, recreation or whatever you do when you ignore obeying the fourth commandment, of honoring the Sabbath? Are you regularly forsaking the assembling of yourself with the saints, to celebrate the creator and honoring God with your tithes and offerings? If so, you are in Babylonian captivity!

The Prophet Haggai exhorted them to repent and make building God's house first priority before their personal pursuits. Praise the Lord, they did, "The remnant of the people, obeyed the voice of the Lord their God." And Haggai prophesied again after their repentance saying, "I am with you says the Lord." He went on to declare God's promise for their obedience, "From this day I will bless you" (Haggai 1:12-13+ 2:19). Then God brought forth the rain they needed to see their crops grow for the harvest.

Now the context of what Haggai said regarding the last days' church was directly affected by what he saw of his own people repenting of the Babylonian spirit of pride and covetousness. He was inspired as he witnessed the people restoring God's house back to its rightful place of first priority. He announced of the last days, "Once more (it is a little while) I will shake the heaven and earth...I will shake all nations, and they shall come to the Desire of All Nations, and I will fill this temple with glory,'... 'The silver is Mine, and the gold is Mine...and the glory of this latter temple shall be greater than the former'...and in this place I will give peace, says the Lord of host!" (Haggai 2:6-9). Yeeha! Mystery Babylon thinks the money belongs to them, it doesn't. It belongs to God. As the shaking of the nations and the revealing of the Anti-Christ draws closer, many of God's people will come to recognize the Babylonian condition of their heart, that it gives Satan a foothold into their lives. They will repent just as Haggai's countrymen did and begin "to seek first the kingdom of God!" When this happens, God will reward the awakened church for sowing anew into the kingdom with reaping the harvest. The glory of the church will be greater than the former. What was the glory of the former? The glory of Solomon's temple was his dominion over the known world of his time. The glory of the latter church will be the admirable saints all over the world, living self controlled lives and rejecting the Anti-Christ's mark and utopian dream. Instead, through faith and patience reflecting the sovereignty of God until the appearance of Jesus Christ and His millennial reign. "In this place I will give peace," said Haggai.

When God's people set their priorities right, missions will flourish, evangelism will prosper, the church will experience unprecedented growth and God's people will be looked upon with admiration by many for the divine character they display. The glory of this latter church will be greater than Solomon's temple.

Significance of Hebrew Names

The Apostle Peter answered Jesus' question, "Whom do you say I am," by proclaiming, "You are the Christ, the Son of the living God." According to Jesus, that revelation does not come from men, it comes from God. It is the precious gift worth dying for. It is the cornerstone of our ability to overcome Satan. Jesus responded, "Upon this rock, I will build my church, and the gates of hell shall not prevail against it" (Matthew 16:16-18). Since that day, Christ has been building His church. The Apostle John observed the strength of the revelation, when he said, "They overcame him by the blood of the Lamb, and by the word of their testimony; and they loved not their lives unto death" (Revelation 12:11). Think of it. We have the capacity through Christ to overcome Satan with the testimony of our revelation. Wow, what a gift!

In the dream of Nebuchadnezzar, Daniel saw "A stone that was cut without hands, which smote the image...and became a great mountain, and filled the whole earth" (Daniel 2:34-35). That stone is the Lord Jesus Christ who is the rock of our salvation. His Lordship in our lives, is the mountain of the church that destroys the image of the beast and Mystery Babylon.

Shadrach, Meshach and Abednego overcame Nebuchadnezzar by refusing to worship the image. They told Nebuchadnezzar they were not anxious about the decision. That God was able to rescue them from the hand of the king, but if he did not, they still would not worship his image. A genuine love for God had formed their character.

Their Hebrew names reveal the influence of God on their lives. Shadrach's original name was Hananiah, it means God has favored. Meshach's Hebrew name was Mishael; it means who or what God is. Abednego's Jewish name was Azariah, it means God has helped. Ironically, their Babylonian names given to them by King Nebuchadnezzar are meaningless.

The truths of their Hebrew names will be the same power working within the Christians of Mystery Babylon, helping us to endure the persecution and overcoming Satan. *God favors us*, we are shining examples of *who or what God is* and *God helps us*. "God has not given us a spirit of fear, but of power and of love, and of a sound mind" (2 Timothy 1:7). Daniel's name means judge of God. During this time of the Anti-Christ, it will be Christ in us the hope of glory that will be the standard by which Mystery Babylon's utopian government will be judged and found lacking.

Daniel concluded his vision of the Anti-Christ's kingdom by declaring, "The Ancient of Days came, and judgment was given to the saints of the most High; and the time came that the saints possessed the kingdom." And "The end of the matter...the saints of the most High shall take the kingdom, and possess the kingdom for ever, even for ever and ever and ever" (Daniel 7:18+21+27-28). Praise the Lord, the end of the matter is God's, and He says we inherit the kingdom. "It's not by power, nor by might, but by my spirit says the Lord" (Zechariah 4:6). His spirit in us prevails and gives us the victory in Jesus Christ.

Chapter 9

Mystery Babylon is Fallen!
"The Day of the Lord"

"Babylon is fallen... that great city, because she has made all nations drink of the wine of the wrath of her fornication." Revelation 14:8

Jesus described His coming, "As it was in the days of Noah, so it will be also in the days of the Son of Man: they ate, they drank, they married wives, they were given in marriage, until the day that Noah entered the ark, and the flood came and destroyed them all" (Luke 17:26-27). One can only imagine society's mindset in Noah's day. After all, no one had ever seen rain before. It was totally foreign to them. They must have laughed old Noah to scorn each time they passed his way, watching him build that boat for a hundred years. He was no doubt the joke of the community, a topic of good chuckles whenever men needed to lighten their spirits. The ancient community was experiencing a great economy, with opportunities abounding. It was the best of times for enjoying pleasure and no one had any thought of impending doom. And then one day it began to rain. From that point, no one was saved except Noah and his family.

The end of Mystery Babylon is very abrupt, just as the end came to Noah's generation. In the fullness of times, God considers the unjust treatment of His saints and decides to bring an end to Mystery Babylon. In the three angels of judgment in Revelation chapter fourteen, the second angel pronounces God's sentence; "Babylon is fallen!" That pronouncement begins the destruction of their world system, punishment and eternal damnation.

The Old Testament prophets referred to this moment by several phrases. The most common phrase is the "day of the Lord." There are several deviations including, "day of the wrath of the Lord," "day of doom," "day of His fierce anger," "day of punishment," "day of the Lord's wrath," "day of the Lord's vengeance" and "day of the Lord's anger." All of these titles pronounce severe judgment and their passages reveal the righteous indignation of God.

The New Testament apostles also speak of this hour with several phrases. Those include: "day of judgment," "day of the Lord," "day of wrath," "day of Christ," "day of Jesus Christ," "day of the Lord Jesus Christ," "that day," "the day," "day of visitation," "day of judgment," "day of God," "judgment of the great day," "great day of His wrath" and the "great day of God almighty." Again, these phrases along with the context of their passages declare judgment on man for his sins and rejection of the Lord. When one studies the entirety these passages, he finds all the days are woven together with several common threads of thought. In this chapter, we will review nine common themes. See Appendix C for scripture references to all of the titles.

Theme #1 Prophesied Against Babylon

The Old Testament prophets were moved by God to pronounce judgment against Babylon for her treatment of Israel. It is interesting that God used Babylon to discipline and correct Israel. The ancient Babylonian kingdom was really nothing more than a puppet in God's hand, to be used by God for his purposes, bringing Israel to a place of repentance and returning to the Lord with all of her heart. Jeremiah declares, "Babylon was a golden cup in the Lord's hand, that made all the earth drunk...Babylon has suddenly fallen and been destroyed" (Jeremiah 51:7-8).

In the same manner, the Anti-Christ of Mystery Babylon is used by God to "Try them, and to purge, and to make them white, even to the time of the end" (Daniel 11:35). The Apostle John said, "The Anti-Christ is coming...by which we know it is the last hour. They went out from us, but they were not of us; for if they had been of us, they would have continued with us; but they went out that they might be manifest, that none of them were of us" (1 John 2:18-19). This is God's way of discerning Christ's true bride, whether she will play the harlot or be faithful. "That He might present it to Himself a glorious church, not having spot or wrinkle, or any such thing, but that it should be holy and without blemish" (Ephesians 5:27). The last day's church truly walks in faith and patience, trusting in Jesus Christ and rejecting the seduction of Mystery Babylon. "Let us be glad and rejoice and give Him glory, for the marriage of the Lamb has come, and His wife has made herself ready" (Revelation 19:2+7-9).

Theme #2 The Trumpet

A familiar refrain concerning the "day of the Lord" is the sounding of the trumpet. Jeremiah (51:27) speaks of this audible event, "blow the trumpet," in his judgments against Babylon. Likewise Zephaniah (1:14-16) and Joel (2:1+15) speak of the same. When the seventh angel and last trumpet is blown in Revelation (11:15), it is immediately announced, "The kingdoms of this world have become the kingdoms of our Lord and of His Christ, and He shall reign forever and ever!" The Apostle Paul confirms the end of the world government, "At His coming, then comes the end, when He delivers the kingdom to God the Father, when He puts an end to all rule and all authority and power" (1 Corinthians 15:23-26).

The Apostle Paul further tells us about the coming of the Lord, "For the Lord Himself will descend from heaven with a shout...with the trumpet of God." Then we are gathered unto the Lord to meet him in the air (1Thessalonians 4:15-17). He also declares, "At His coming...in a moment, in the twinkling of an eye, at the last trumpet. For the trumpet will sound, and the dead will be raised...." (1 Corinthians 15:23+52).

At this point, something very wonderful happens for the saints. We are forever with the Lord (1Thessalonians 4:17-18). This is very comforting for three reasons. The entirety of our Christian life has been a walk of faith. We have never seen the Lord, instead we follow his spirit, but now we see him face to face. Secondly, when the trumpet is blown the mystery of God is finished (Revelation 10:7). No longer are we seeing through a glass darkly, for now we know and understand just as God knows us. There are no more puzzles to figure out, we fully understand everything God was saying through the prophets. Thirdly, the unsaved fully understand as well, because they immediately cry out for the rocks and the mountains to fall upon them to hide them from the "day of the Lord." See theme #5.

Many well meaning Christians separate the rapture (our gathering together to meet the Lord in the air) out from the "day of the Lord." The rapture is clearly a part of the last trump (1 Corinthians 15:51-54) and the last trump is clearly a part of the "day of the Lord" (Revelation 11:15). Furthermore, the Apostle John says that when the seventh Angel is about to sound his trumpet, "The mystery of God would be finished, as He declared to His servants the prophets" (Revelation 10:7). If the rapture is a prior, separate event from the "day of the Lord," there is still a lot of mystery to be discovered by those left behind. They will be trying to discern what the prophets were saying about God and the last days and where did all these people disappear too? Is it possible the rapture and the "day of the Lord" are the same event? I believe it is and we will learn more about this in chapter eleven.

Theme #3 No More Death for the Saints

The Apostle Paul proclaims in the "day of the Lord," "The last enemy that will be destroyed is death...then shall be brought to pass the saying that is written: Death is swallowed up in victory" (1 Corinthians 15:26+54). Paul is quoting Isaiah 25:8-9. Through out Isaiah's writings, he only speaks of one "day of the Lord". No wonder Paul jubilantly rejoices, "Thanks be to God who gives us the victory through our Lord Jesus Christ." And admonishes, "Therefore, my beloved brethren, be steadfast, immovable, always abounding in the work of the Lord, knowing that your labor is not in vain in the Lord" (1 Corinthians 15:57-58). Once the "day of the Lord" takes place, Christians will never again suffer death.

Theme #4 Judgment is Quick

Isaiah says of Babylon's judgment, "In a moment, in one day...." (47:1+9). Paul said it is in the twinkling of an eye..." (1Corinthians 15:52). Jeremiah (51:8) says it is sudden. The Apostle John says it happens to Mystery Babylon in "one hour" (Revelation 18:10).   Jesus is asked by his disciples, "What will be the sign of your coming, and the end of the age?" Jesus replies, "For as the lighting comes from the east and flashes to the west, so also will the coming of the Son of Man be" (Matthew 24:3+27).   Everyone has been in a thunderstorm and experienced the flash and pop of lighting. If a house is struck by lighting, everything collapses, TV, computers, lights, clocks, and electricity. Likewise, the return of Jesus on the "day of the Lord" will take place instantly and God will destroy the worldwide kingdom of Mystery Babylon.

Theme #5
Men Cry for Rocks and Mountains to Fall on Them

When Christ is revealed from heaven, just as the mystery of God is finished for us, so the mystery is finished for the unsaved. Instantly they realize, OOPS we have made a mistake in our assumptions. The realization is one of horror; they persecuted Christians and worshipped the Anti-Christ in ignorant deception. Isaiah describes their plight; "They shall go into the holes of the rocks, and into the caves of the earth, from the terror of the Lord and the glory of His majesty, when He arises to shake the earth mightily" (Isaiah 2:19-21). The Apostle John describes the same scenario (Revelation 6:12-17). As Jesus was being led to crucifixion, He no doubt was thinking about the coming judgment of God to exact justice when He said, "The days are coming in which they will say, ... to the mountains, 'fall on us! and to the hills, cover us!'" (Luke 23:29-30).

Theme #6 Their Wealth Can't Help

The Prophet Ezekial declares, "They will throw their silver into the streets, and their gold will be like refuse; their silver and gold will not be able to deliver them in the day of the wrath of the Lord" (Ezekial7:19). This "day of the Lord" is indeed traumatic, because I can't imagine anything that would cause people to come up off their riches in such fashion. After all, wealth is their security blanket in life. Is it possible that men will think to themselves, fortune is what caused me to reject God for the Anti-Christ, maybe God will believe I am repenting when He sees me tossing material wealth like garbage? Zephaniah and Isaiah echo the same prophetic truth (Zephaniah 1:11+14+18 Isaiah 2:19-21).

James the brother of Jesus bemoans, "Come now you rich, weep and howl for your miseries that are coming on you! Your riches...your gold and silver...will be a witness against you and will eat your flesh like fire. You have heaped up treasure in the last days...You have lived on the earth in pleasure and luxury; you have fattened your hearts as in a day of slaughter" (James5:1-7). The Apostle John describes their pursuit of affluence as the reason for God's judgment and their fate was sealed the moment they took the mark of the beast (Revelation 14:9-11). The entire chapter of Revelation 18 is a picture of the worthlessness of goods in the hour of God's judgment. The "day of the Lord" is a climatic event that dispels any notion of the bumper sticker, "In the end, he that has the most toys wins."

Theme #7 As Sodom

The Pharisees asked Jesus, when the kingdom of God

would come? He replied, "As it was...in the days of Lot: They ate, they drank, they bought, they sold, they planted, they built; but on the day that Lot went out of Sodom it rained fire and brimstone from heaven and destroyed them all. Even so will it be in the day when the Son of Man is revealed" (Luke 17:20+28-30).

Men are so busy with their lives; they do not have the slightest inclination of any impending doom. Their lifestyles are filled with economic opportunity and they are hurrying about enjoying the pleasures of the day. However, of enormous concern to anyone with an unsaved love one, "is fire and brimstone destroys them all." No one is allowed to repent or get right with God once the "day of the Lord" begins. This alone should cause everyone to re-examine the scriptures carefully, so they may be persuaded concerning the "day of the Lord" and share their faith with zeal. Jesus' statement about Sodom and hell fire on the "day of the Lord" is bolstered by Isaiah (13:1+19), Jeremiah (50:40) and the letter written to Jude (6-7).

Theme #8 Hell is their Reward

Isaiah foretells the doom awaiting those who are judged by God in the "day of the Lord's vengeance." He describes that day as brimstone that is never quenched (Isaiah 34:1-4+8-10). The Book of Jude reverberates, "suffering the vengeance of eternal fire" (Jude 6-7). Likewise, the Apostle John says the inhabitants of Mystery Babylon who took the mark of the beast will be "tormented with fire and brimstone...forever and ever" (Revelation 14:9-11).

The Apostle Peter warns of the judgment of fire, "The elements will melt with fervent heat; both the earth and the works that are in it will be burned up. Therefore, since all these things will be dissolved, what manner of persons ought you to be in holy conduct and godliness, looking for and hastening the day of God" (2 Peter 3:10-12). Yet men laugh and mock the Christian, confidant that we are deluded with fairy tales. As they treated Noah, they will also treat Christians.

Theme #9 The Sun, the Moon and the Stars

One of the most fascinating and prolific threads woven throughout the prophetic utterances of the "day of the Lord" is the loss of light by the sun, moon and stars. The Book of Genesis tells about the sun, moon and stars on the fourth day of creation and mentions their purpose are not just to give light, but to "be for signs and seasons...." (Genesis 1:14-19). Through these great heavenly bodies, God communicates his purposes.

Solomon acknowledges a principle of God's favor on His people as long as these heavenly bodies exist (Psalms 72:5-7). Psalmist Ethan declares the covenant of the Lord with His servant David is as the sun and the moon before God (Psalm 89:34-37). Just as the rainbow is a sign God will never judge the earth with a flood again; the sun and the moon are reminders of the Lord's favor to the nation of Israel.

Solomon warns, "Remember now your Creator in the days of your youth, before the difficult days come, and the years draw near when you say, 'I have no pleasure in them': while the sun and the light, the moon and the stars, are not darkened...." (Ecclesiastes 12:1-2). It is almost as if he is saying we have a window of opportunity to experience God's wonderful grace and mercy, take advantage of it while you can.   The Prophet Joel says exactly that. He admonishes God's people to get right with their maker, while he is full of grace and mercy, for the time is coming when the sun, moon and stars will grow dark and His kindness will be given way to judgment of wrath   (Joel 2:10-13). This new testament season of mercy is known to theologians as the church age or the age of grace. It is the time period from the birth of the church till the time of God's judgment (Joel 2:28-32 + 3:14-16, Acts 2:12-21).

Ironically, Solomon's admonitions to the Hebrews came to pass when the sun was darkened in the middle of the day when Jesus was crucified (Luke 23:44-45). The veil of the temple was split from top to bottom, signifying God's extended grace to the gentiles. But it also represented the judgment of Israel for having rejected their messiah.

Isaiah proclaims the judgment sign of the sun, moon and stars in his prophecy towards Babylon. He does this in chapter thirteen (v.1+6-12) and chapter twenty-four (v.19-23). Then in chapter twenty-five Isaiah says, "He will swallow up death forever, and the Lord will wipe away tears from all faces; the rebuke of His people, He will take away from all the earth...and it will be said in that day: 'behold, this is our God; we have waited for Him, and He will save us. This is the Lord; we have waited for Him; we will be glad and rejoice in His salvation" (Isaiah 25:8-9). The Apostle Paul quotes this passage in the context of the Lord's coming, "In a moment, in the twinkling of an eye, at the last trumpet. For the trumpet will sound...then shall be brought to pass the saying that is written: 'Death is swallowed up in victory'" (1 Corinthians 15:52+54).

Jesus' disciples ask this question, "What will be the sign of your coming, and of the end of the age?" Jesus answered, "Immediately after the tribulation of those days the sun will be darkened, and the moon will not give its light; the stars will fall from heaven, and the powers of the heavens will be shaken. Then the sign of the Son of Man will appear in heaven, and then all the tribes of the earth will mourn, and they will see the Son of Man coming on the clouds of heaven with power and great glory. And He will send His angels with a great sound of a trumpet, and they will gather together His elect from the four winds, from one end of heaven to the other" (Matthew 24:3+29-31). This sign of the darkened sun, moon and stars is expressed in Mark (13:4+24-27) and Luke (17:21:7+25-27) as well.

In "The Revelation of Jesus Christ, which God gave Him to show His servants-things which must shortly take place" (Revelation 1:1), the Apostle John saw the same sign concerning the sun, moon and stars losing their light, as part of "the great day of His wrath" (Revelation 6:12-17). Jesus said, "When you see these things begin to happen, look up and lift up your heads, because your redemption draws nears" (Luke 21:28). When the sun moon and stars begin to loose their light, God will be speaking to His people that Christ's return is imminent. It will be a welcomed sign to the saints who are being persecuted.

The Judgement of Babylon

When one considers all of the passages centered on the phrase, "day of the Lord," it becomes apparent that God decides in the fullness of times to cut short the abominations of Babylon. He judged the Old Testament Babylon for their cruelty toward His people Israel. In like manner, He will judge Mystery Babylon for their cruelty to the saints. Babylon is indeed a "cup in the Lord's hand," for once she accomplishes God's purpose, God brings forth His wrath on her for the cruelty she displayed towards the saints.

Chapter 10

The Wrath of the Lamb!
"God's Outpouring of Punishment"

"It is a righteous thing with God to repay with tribulation those who trouble you." 2 Thessalonians 1:6

In discussing the great tribulation, it is important to distinguish between tribulation and wrath. Tribulation always refers to man's persecution of saints for their faith in Jesus Christ. However, the tribulation of God always refers to the wrath of God towards men who unjustly persecute God's people. God is emphatic in His writings through the Apostle Paul, "For God did not appoint us to wrath, but to obtain salvation through our Lord Jesus Christ" (1 Thessalonians 5:9).

The history of the Roman persecution of the early New Testament church, along with *Fox's Book of Martyrs* is evidence enough that Christians have endured tribulation for their love of Jesus throughout history. Even today persecution is commonly reported by missionaries, of Christians who are treated with cruelty in China and born-again Muslims who are executed for disgracing their families by turning to Christ. These tribulations and others will only intensify in the latter days.

However, there is great controversy over the presence of saints during the outpouring of God's wrath. The wrath of God is expressed in the seals, trumpets and bowls of "The Revelation of Jesus Christ." Christians are never the objects of the wrath of God; instead it is the ungodly and their unjust treatment of Christians that is the reason for God's unleashing of wrath. His punishment is focused on those who refuse His will and persecuted the saints. So the question is begged, are Christians present when God pours out His wrath on the unjust? For all the controversy surrounding this question within the body of Christ, there is a reasonable answer and explanation.

Throughout the scriptures, God has poured out His wrath in several theaters of human punishments. The flood of Noah, the fire and brimstone of Sodom and Gomorrah, the ten plagues of Egypt, the killing of the firstborn of Pharaoh's kingdom and the parting of the Red Sea. In each out pouring of wrath, God's people were present. Noah was secure in the ark as the rain came down for forty days and forty nights. Abraham viewed from a distance, the smoke of Sodom and Gomorrah. The children of Israel were safely in Goshen during the ten plagues of Egypt, enjoying the protection of God. God told Pharaoh, "In that day I will set apart the land of Goshen, in which my people dwell...I will make a difference between My people and your people" (Exodus 8:22-23). The Israelites were behind the blood stained door posts and lintels of their homes when the death angel struck the firstborn of Egypt. And Israel sang the song of Moses as they witnessed the collapsing of the Red Sea, which drown the army of Pharaoh.

These days, news reporters stand in the midst of hurricanes, capturing live TV shots of nature's fury. In the Gulf War, we saw them on top of buildings in Baghdad, as they got the story of smart bombs and cruise missiles crashing and exploding in full sight of their cameras, exacting their vengeance on surgically targeted military sights. If the technology of man allows news personnel to confidently brush with disaster to get the scoop, then God who allowed Moses to walk through the plague of hail and brimstone   (Exodus 9:24-33) and secured His people in former days of wrath, will safely protect us as we witness the out pouring of God's wrath on a disobedient generation in the last days.

Though Christians are never the objects of God's wrath, there are several passages that persuade me that the saints will be present during the outpouring of God's punishment on the Anti-Christ and Mystery Babylon. Here are four scriptural reasons why Christians will be present during the outpouring of God's wrath.

First, "The Book of Revelation" is about the revealing of Jesus Christ. Jesus is the one opening the seven seals. It is not until the sixth seal that we see the sign of the sun, moon and stars and the appearance of the "day of the Lord" (Revelation 5:5, 6:1+12-17). Therefore, Jesus has poured out on the earth five of the seals before He reveals Himself in the sixth seal. The first four seals are the four horsemen of the Apocalypse, which are the four spirits of heaven sent out from the Lord to the earth (Zechariah 6:2-5, Revelation 6:1-8). The last three seals are the results of these spirits influencing the earth and the saints are clearly a part of them. The entire premise of this book can be seen in these seven seals. See Appendix D. The opening of the seventh seal is simply the revealing of the seven trumpets. The angels pour out the wrath of their six trumpets, before Jesus is revealed at the seventh and last trump (Revelation 11:15).

Secondly, the fifth trumpet is an unleashing of locust that has scorpion like powers to torment men. They are given specific instructions to harm only those men who are not sealed by God. The men who are sealed by God are certainly righteous people or why would God protect them?   (Revelation 9:4-5). The reason is the saints are present during this plague.

Third, the Apostle John notes carnal men refuse to repent in spite of God's plagues. Obviously, this would not be applicable unless there was an opportunity for them to repent. This notation is during the plagues of the fourth bowl, fifth bowl and sixth trumpet (Revelation 9:20-21, 16:9+11). Once the "day of the Lord" comes, there remains no more opportunity to repent (Luke 17:29-30). Therefore, these plagues must be before the appearing of Jesus at the "day of the Lord."

Lastly, the Apostle John sees a sign in heaven, seven angels who have the last seven plagues completing the wrath of God. These angels come from the temple of God and it is observed that no one may enter the temple until the plagues are completed. It is after the angels with the last seven plagues are revealed that, "Those who have the victory over the beast, over his image and over his mark," appear singing, "the song of Moses" (Revelation 15:1-8). Their song is one of extolling God for His great and marvelous works, His name and His judgments. This sign is parallel to the rejoicing Hebrews of the Exodus who came through the plagues of Egypt untouched and witnessed Pharaoh's army being judged at the Red Sea (Exodus 15:1-18). They too sing the song of Moses, rejoicing in God who overthrew their enemies with His wrath.

Plagues of Exodus and Revelation Paralleled

The Israelites of the Exodus safely dwelt in Goshen, enduring the very same plagues mentioned in Revelation. With the exception of the fourth bowl, which is scorching heat, the sixth trumpet, which is the two hundred million-man army and the third trumpet which is bitter water, the experience of plagues is the same. If the mighty army of

Pharaoh described in Exodus parallels the army of Revelation and the bloody waters of Exodus correspond to the bitter water of Revelation, then scorching heat is the only plague of Revelation the Jews of Exodus did not experience while secure in Goshen. See Appendix E. It is extremely difficult to make a case for the saints not being present during the great tribulation, solely on the basis of the wrath of God, when Godly men have been present during the very same plagues in historical events of the past.

So why and to what purpose would God desire saints to endure these traumatic events directed against Mystery Babylon and the Anti-Christ? I believe it is for the same reasons concerning His salvation of the Jews from Egypt. God stated of Pharaoh, "For this time I will send all My plagues...that you may know there is none like me in all the earth...for this purpose I have raised you up, that I may show My power in you, and that My name may be declared in all the earth" (Exodus 9:14+16). God was preparing His nation of Israel to enter the land of Canaan with the knowledge of His mighty power.   Likewise, God uses the Anti-Christ to prepare His saints for the millennial kingdom, emphasizing to them His magnificence as our Savior. God exalts Himself one last time at the close of the age to let the saints know of His preeminence as He prepares them to reign and rule with Him in the kingdom of peace.

Chapter 11

Pre-Trib Rapture Ramifications
"And Destroyed Them All"

*"As it was in the days of Noah, so it will be in the days of
the Son of Man: they ate, they drank, they married wives,
they were given in marriage, until the flood came and
destroyed them all." Luke 17:26-27*

The prevailing view of the rapture is: no one knows the
day or the hour of Jesus' appearance. Suddenly Christians
disappear and through this magnificent event, people
begin to ponder, search and turn to the Lord. The Anti-
Christ is then revealed because the Holy Spirit is no
longer holding him back. Others add, there are one
hundred and forty four thousand Jews left behind to be
witnesses and through their preaching they convert a
multitude to Christ. There are enormous ramifications
associated with a clear understanding of the rapture.
Therefore we must rethink, reconsider and lay before the
Lordship of Christ our hopeful views and instead cleave
to a scriptural perspective.

Although the word rapture never occurs in the
scriptures, its idea or meaning does. It simply means to be
taken, transported or snatched away with joy and
exultation. This rescue is the same truth centered on the
"day of the Lord." For some reason, men have separated
the idea of the rapture from the "day of the Lord," as if
they are two separate events. This is contrary to Paul's
writings. Consider his letter to Corinth, "So that
you...waiting for the revelation of our Lord Jesus Christ,
who will confirm you to the end, that you may be
blameless in the day of our Lord Jesus Christ" (1

Corinthians 1:7-8). The end is the revealing of Jesus Christ! And He strengthens us right up to that moment called the "day of our Lord Jesus Christ." They are not two separate events, but one in the same.

Escapism Mentality

The danger I sense with this separation of the rapture, is the idea of escapism to the exclusion of genuine growth in faith and patience. It seems Christians are embracing Christ as savior, but not His lordship in their approach to the rapture. Salvation without lordship is like a motor without oil. The engine will start and run, but seizes when the heat builds. If God tarries until after the revealing of the Anti-Christ, as the scriptures say He will, then Christians are going to need the character of Christ to withstand the pressure to take the mark, that would cause their loss of salvation (Revelation 14:9-12). This character only comes from following Jesus' lordship. It does not come as a gospel pill, that you swallow and instantaneously become super saints ready to withstand the enemy. Instead, we must have vision to look carefully into the future with honest hearts and begin to prepare ourselves according to the Wisdom of Solomon, "A prudent man foresees evil and hides himself, but the simple pass on and are punished" (Proverbs 22:3). This character is developed by standing behind the shield of faith, putting on the whole armor of God.

If one is persuaded the rapture is prior to the revealing of the Anti-Christ, then he might assume that missing church is no worse than cutting classes at college. He'll just make it up the next time he visits. After all, no one knows the day or hour and life continues just as it always has. There are things to do in this busy life. Besides God accepts him just the way he is. One can sense the laziness in this attitude. However, if one is persuaded the days are coming in which you will face the greatest tribulation known to man (Matthew 24:21), then one grasps the gravity of being faithful in the house of the Lord. There is no time to lose as we prepare ourselves for increasing darkness. Like infantry in the military preparing to be deployed within twenty-four hours to the front lines of battle, they continually train and exercise their skills to be combat ready. Likewise, soldiers of Christ because of such genuine spiritual preparation are truly ready for the imminent return of Jesus at the "day of the Lord."

The Apostle Paul sees faith and patience as essential for enduring the tribulation of men. He did not approach the "day of the Lord" as an escapism ideology; instead he saw it as place of rest for all that come through the tribulation of men. Paul says, "We ourselves boast of you among the churches of God for your patience and faith in all your persecutions and tribulations that you endure, which is manifest evidence of the righteous judgment of God, that you may be counted worthy of the kingdom of God, for which you also suffer; ...and give you who are troubled rest with us when the Lord Jesus is revealed from heaven...when He comes, in that Day, to be glorified in His saints and to be admired among all who believe...." (2 Thessalonians 1:4-10).

God did not give us grace to escape doing the will of God; He gave grace to enable us to obey His will with faithfulness and perseverance. We must avail ourselves of that grace by faithfully attending to the Word and Spirit of the Lord. Paul said, "I do not frustrate the grace of God...." (Galations2: 21). Grace is the agent of personal relationship that emboldens us to grow from being mere "babes in Christ" to being "more than conquerors!"

Lethargy in Evangelism

The Rev. Billy Graham once shared a frightening statistic, that less than five percent of Christians ever share their faith and lead someone to Christ. This is tragic and yet totally understandable, for people will logically deduct from the prevailing view of the rapture, there is no reason to endure rejection for sharing one's faith. After all, when the rapture takes place they will see the truth and turn to the Lord, because of the overwhelming evidence of the absence of Christians. This sounds totally reasonable and yet it is totally wrong. These people are victims of misinformation.

Jesus Christ said, "No one can come to Me unless the Father who sent Me draws him" (John 6:44). The agent by which the Father draws men is the Holy Spirit, who convicts of sin. If the Holy Spirit is taken out during a separate rapture, how will people be convicted and drawn to the Lord? And when you study the one hundred and forty four thousand marked Jews, who supposedly are leading all these people to Christ, where are the converted when they reappear with the Lamb on Mount Zion in Revelation chapter 14 ? There aren't any!

The scriptures clearly teach the "day of the Lord" is, as it was in the days of Noah and Lot. Who was saved after the flood of Noah? Who was saved in Sodom after the fire and brimstone fell? No one! In the "day of the Lord", many will perish because Christians forfeited their spiritual responsibility to share their faith over a lack of understanding of the scriptures and fear of rejection. This separate rapture idea is encouraging lethargy.

Revival never occurs from proving one's position anyway. For winning an argument will change one's intellect, but will never change one's heart. Revival happens when we understand the price of laying down our lives. That price is following the example of Christ who suffered the persecution of the cross and endured the tribulation of men. Likewise, Christians will follow the example of Christ by living humbly and rejecting the covetous ways of Mystery Babylon. As we endure ill treatment at the hands of the unjust, men's hearts will be moved with righteous indignation and desire to follow the spirit of truth, rather than the popular opinions of men. Then true revival will occur, for this is the same spirit that leads us to Christ.

Jesus said, "I have a baptism to be baptized with; and how am I straitened till it be accomplished!" (Luke 12:50). Jesus understood His future and gathered Himself to submit to the Father's will for His life. His example was prophesied, "He was oppressed and He was afflicted...He was led as a lamb to the slaughter, and as a sheep before its shearers is silent, so He opened not His mouth" (Isaiah 53:7, Matthew 26:63, 27:12-14). It was His humble submission to the Father's will, that causes men to desire the same character and strength which can only be gotten by daily bearing the lordship of His cross.

Jesus told His disciples, "I still have many things to say to you, but you cannot bear them now." When the disciples quizzed Him further, Jesus responded. "You will weep and lament, but the world will rejoice; and you will be sorrowful, but your sorrow will turn to joy...therefore you now have sorrow; but I will see you again and your heart will rejoice, and your joy no one will take from you" (John 16:12+20+22). This not only describes Jesus being taken from them and their ultimate reunion at His resurrection, but it also describes the last day's generation. For just as the disciples bore the baptism of martyrdom, looking for the hope of His return, so we will endure the persecution of Mystery Babylon looking for His return. Consider the lyrics of Christian music and worship over the past decade. Much of it has been about God preparing His army and Christians fighting battles and reigning victorious through Christ. These are not physical battles, for the Apostle John warned in the time of the Anti-Christ, "He who kills with the sword, must be killed with the sword. Here is the patience of the saints" (Revelation 13:10). Jesus said, "My kingdom is not of this world. If My kingdom were of this world, My servants would fight, so I should not be delivered to the Jews; but My kingdom is not from here" (John 18:36). The warfare referred to in our Christian songs is the battle of faith and patience. The battle is exercising self-control and subduing our carnal flesh. This means getting victory to walk in the character of our Lord and demonstrating to the world the true King of Kings. How? By submitting ourselves to God in heaven and not to the Anti-Christ god of Mystery Babylon.

It is the example of saints, who lay down their lives as Christ did, that brings revival. The early disciples proclaimed the salvation of the Lord, so man would not perish in following the world to destruction. It resulted in the world being turned upside down. Because of the proper evangelism perspective of the last day's saints, "The earth will be filled with the knowledge of the Lord, as the waters cover the seas" (Habakkuk 2:14).

The entirety of this book is dedicated to motivating Christians to realize the subtle influence of Mystery Babylon upon their lives. To inspire them to shake free of its seduction through repentance, by dying to covetousness, as oppose to following the popular opinions of the world to their destruction.

No One Knows vs. Had You Known the Hour

Daniel came to understand from the reading of the Prophet Jeremiah, that the Babylonian captivity of Israel would be seventy years (Daniel 9:2). If he grasped the writings of Jeremiah, it is reasonable to assume he also understood from the writings of Isaiah, that Cyrus would come to power and during his reign, the Isralites would be set free to return to Jerusalem (Isaiah 44:26-28+45:1, Daniel 10:1). Just as Daniel came to know the timing of their release in number of years and under the reigning King Cyrus in ancient Babylon, it is reasonable for Christians in Mystery Babylon to know the season of our Lord's return. And who the Anti-Christ is when the "day of the Lord" comes.

Jesus challenged the Pharisees of His day saying, "When it is evening you will say, 'it will be fair weather, for the sky is red'; "and in the morning, 'it will be foul weather today, for the sky is red and threatening.'... You know how to discern the face of the sky, but you cannot discern the signs of the times" (Matthew 16:2-3). Jesus acknowledged their accurate assessments of the weather and chided them for not understanding the signs of the spiritual seasons. He fully expected them to know the signs of the times, just as they understood predicting weather. Today Doppler weather forecasts can actually show us through radar the approaching cold and warm fronts. Weathermen accurately predict the five-day forecasts of sun and rain along with temperatures to within a few degrees. In these last days, Jesus gives the opportunity to understand the signs of the times at least as well as Daniel.

People constantly affirm concerning the Lord's return, "Of that day and hour, no one knows, not even the angels of heaven, but My Father only." They quote Jesus' words, "Watch therefore, for you do not know what hour your Lord is coming" (Matthew 24:36+42). I agree with Jesus. We do not know the exact day or hour. I would never set a day or hour as many have in the past. Date setting is ridiculous and detrimental to the Christian faith. Many harms have come from those who have done so in the past.

But this does not mean we can't know the season! The word hour in the Greek, pronounced ho'rah is used consistently throughout the New Testament and it means, literally or figuratively, instant, hour, day, or season. Jesus said we do not know the instant, hour or day. But He expects us to know the season! Consider Jesus' admonishments to the church in Sardis, "Remember therefore how you have received and heard; hold fast and repent. Therefore if you will not watch, I will come upon you as a thief, and you will not know what hour I will come upon you" (Revelation 3:3). In this passage, Jesus is encouraging us to walk in repentance so *we may know the hour* of his coming. Since we don't know the instant, hour or day, he must be talking about the season with really close accuracy, just as Daniel understood their release from ancient Babylon.

Jesus further says, "If the master of the house had known what hour the thief would come, he would have watched and not allowed his house to be broken into" (Luke 12:39). My neighbors tell me their houses were broken into frequently before we moved to our present location. The reason is because no one is ever home. Both parents work and their dwellings are empty and inviting. Because Linda is a housewife who home schools our children, someone is always running and playing in the yards and their mere presence discourages burglars. No burglar is going to visit under those conditions. Jesus said the key to knowing the hour or season is to walk in a repentant lifestyle towards the Lord. Jesus reiterates, "Behold I am coming as a thief. Blessed is he who watches, and keeps his garments, lest he walk naked and they see his shame" (Revelation 16:15). His coming as a thief is only to those who walk unrepentant. To those who live for God, they are blessed because they know the hour or season!

The Season

One obvious sign of the times will be the revealing of the Anti-Christ. When the Anti-Christ definitively manifests himself with the implementation of the mark, so no one will be able to buy or sell without the mark, this will indicate the "day of the Lord" is close (2 Thessalonians 2:3).

Another sign of tremendous importance is Jerusalem. Jesus said, "Jerusalem will be trampled by the Gentiles until the times of the Gentiles are fulfilled." He then adds, "This generation will by no means pass away till all things take place. Heaven and earth will pass away, but My words will by no means pass away" (Luke 21:24+32-33). Jerusalem was under the divided control of both Palestine and Israel until the six-day war of 1967. At that time Israel defeated her neighboring Arab states and recaptured control over the previously divided city, bringing the city under Jewish dominance.

According to Jesus, this generation will not pass away until all things are finished. But what is a generation? Many have said it is about twenty years, because this is how long it takes for a child to grow to an adult. Others say forty years, because this is the number of years for

judgment. Such as forty years of wandering in the desert
or forty days and nights in Noah's flood. Still others say
about seventy years, for this is how long God promised
man to live in a lifetime.

The time frame for a generation that I am comfortable
with is between one hundred years and one hundred and
seven and one half years. Why this number? When God
was making covenant with Abraham, He declared his
descendants would be in captivity four hundred years. He
then announced they would return to Canaan in the fourth
generation (Genesis 15:12-16). A quarter of four
centuries would be one hundred years. So why do I add
the seven and a half years? Simple, the Israelites were
actually in Egypt four hundred and thirty years (Exodus
12:40). One fourth of thirty is seven and one half years,
thus rendering the fourth generation to a maximum total
of one hundred and seven and one half years. As a child
of Abraham, I am comfortable with this time frame.
Using this generation time period, the "day of the Lord"
will be taking place between now and approximately
2075 AD. This is not a declaration of the day or hour,
but recognition of our present season. It is a reasonable
assessment of the scriptures and a discerning of the signs
of the times. God is sovereign and can do anything He
wants. He could allow Jerusalem to fall victim to her
Gentile enemies, in which case I am adding the
generation years to the wrong date and would have to
reassess. But presently, Jerusalem is no longer under
Gentile control.

Microchip technology is rapidly bringing mankind to
the time of implementing the universal personal
identification code. This will be a result of the
cooperation of the nations, making way for a world
market place in which no one may buy or sell without the

mark. The implanting of the mark will be the definitive revealing of the Anti-Christ. There is ample time between now and 2075A.D. for this event and the technology to be arrayed. It is also within the scope of a generation from the time Jerusalem was brought under the dominion of Israel. Heck, another godless system called communism rose and fell in only seventy years in the past century. So it is reasonable to believe the convergence of science and prophecy is like the receding sands of an hourglass, bringing us to the precipice of the "day of the Lord."

Just as Daniel understood the season of 70 years of Babylonian captivity and their being released during the reign of King Cyrus, so it is possible for Christians to understand the season of our release from Mystery Babylon.

Signs of the Times

It is paramount that the church understands the horizon of future events, to protect itself from the malaise of apathy and entrapment of Mystery Babylon. During the next several decades, the church will experience several pervading influences drawing us to the "day of the Lord." There will be the continued rise of the covetous spirit of Mystery Babylon, the disdain of the lost, saying "where is the promise of His coming?", the talk of implementing the UPIC, the great falling away of luke warm saints, the great revival, the revealing of the Anti-Christ with tribulations toward the church and the outpouring of God's wrath on the lost.

The idea of being raptured before the revealing of the Anti-Christ and the great tribulation is comforting to my flesh. I like the idea. However, when I consider the faithfulness and patience of the saints who are martyred in Revelation during the time of the Anti-Christ, I have to ask myself, who are these guys? I must ask the pre-Anti-Christ rapture theorists, how they became so strong in their convictions, demonstrating such incredible character and strength, especially in the short time between the rapture and the revealing of the Anti-Christ. A twinge of jealously comes to my spirit as I realize this is the kind of Christian I have always wanted to be. Pure in my love for God, without spot or blemish, more than a conqueror as I represent the kingdom of my Lord Jesus Christ! Just like an athlete who has always longed to be on a championship team under the tutoring of a great coach. Then I realize, I have been robbed of the opportunity to be honed and sharpened in my character by the popular but lethargic pre-Anti-Christ rapture.

Then I awaken to the truth, God did not call these fictional Christians to purity, He calls us to purity. We are those Christians. We are the victorious saints. Like the underdog fighter Rocky, we are trained by the Spirit to put on the whole armor of God. He leads us through the training sessions of these last days, purifying our hearts until we are ready to quench all the fiery darts of the devil with the shield of faith. "Therefore, ...let us lay aside every weight, and the sin which so easily ensnares us, and let us run with endurance the race that is set before us, looking unto Jesus, the author and finisher of our faith, who for the joy that was set before Him, endured the cross, despising the shame, and has sat down at the right hand of the throne of God" (Hebrews 12:1-2). As a Christian, I am looking for the revealing of Christ at the end of the race. Until then, Jesus is more than able to finish and perfect my faith as I follow His example. If the Lord should tarry, I will be ready for His appearing because I have resolved to take up His cross and love not my life unto death!

Chapter 12

The Repentant Babylonian Captives
"Following Their Example!"

"Therefore, since all these things will be dissolved, what manner of persons ought you to be in holy conduct and godliness, looking for and hastening the coming of the day of God, because of which the heavens will be dissolved, being on fire, and the elements will melt with fervent heat?" 2 Peter 3:11-12

When Daniel understood the years of Israel's captivity by the writings of Jeremiah, he began to seek the Lord in prayer and fasting. He approached God according to the Lord's character of mercy. He prayed, "We have sinned and committed iniquity, we have done wickedly and rebelled, even by departing from Your precepts and Your judgments. Neither have we heeded Your servants the prophets, who spoke in Your name...." Daniel then acknowledges God's just punishment of Israel was because of "unfaithfulness" (Daniel 9:5-7).

The beginnings of Israel's release from captivity were propelled by a righteous intercessor that identified with Israel's sins. Note how Daniel prays "we" throughout his seeking of God. This righteous prophet understood God's requirements of intercession, "Then shall you call, and the Lord will answer, you shall cry, and He will say, 'here I am.' If you take away the yoke from your midst, the pointing of the finger...and...those among you shall build the old waste places; you shall raise up the foundations of many generations; and you shall be called the Repairer of the Breach, The Restorer of Streets to Dwell In" (Isaiah 58:9+12).

Daniel's humble confessions and identification with the sins of his country began the restoration of Israel and the rebuilding of the Holy City of Jerusalem. He did not point the finger at other men's sins, but identified with them.

The books of Ezra and Nehemiah reveal the leadership of Daniel's contemporaries in the restoration process. Their example of repentance is the same that America's Christian leaders must follow if we are to see the body of Christ return to its effectiveness as salt and light. We can not point the finger at one another's denominational affiliation, the failure of a political party or world government. We must begin to acknowledge our participation and repentance from the sins that took Israel captive to Babylon, for they are the same that have taken us captive into Mystery Babylon. If we are to see the resurgence of the church in America, we must repent of the sins described in Ezra and Nehemiah.

The Temple's Foundation

Upon returning to Jerusalem, their first chore was to rebuild the foundations of the temple. The temple was the center of their relationship with God. The ruins of the foundation were the result of the invading Babylonians and were symbolic of the Jews' former backsliding. The writer of Hebrews describes the foundations of Christian belief. "Therefore, leaving the discussion of the elementary principles of Christ, let us go on to perfection, not laying again the foundation of repentance from dead works and of faith toward God, of the doctrine of baptisms... of resurrection of the dead, and of eternal judgement" (Hebrews 6:1-2).

Mystery Babylon attacks these foundations in our

Christian walk and seeks to undermine our convictions with apathy. We must return to the sobering reality that there is a judgement day, in which men will be resurrected and held accountable with eternal consequences before God for their behavior. Repentance from all our carnal activities is paramount to exercising faith towards God. Only then can we be assured of going on to perfection in Christ Jesus.

Perhaps a reminder to the body of Christ of the importance of foundation is the ancient city of Venice, Italy, which is literally sinking. The island community of Venice is ironically shaped like a fish. It was built on a lagoon and acquired religious significance when the bones of saint San Marco were smuggled to the city, to be enshrined in the ninth century. Ancient Venice was an economic trading power in the east west exchange of goods. Today, Venice is no longer a trading empire, instead it survives off the tourist trade of those seeking a romantic gondola ride down the canals of the city, to observe the rising watermark of the sinking architecture. If our relationship to Christ degenerates into the apathetic worship of dead bones and mere religious ceremony, as we plunge ourselves into the commerce of Mystery Babylon, we are sunk as Christians. We must remember the significance of our water baptism, to be identified in the likeness of Jesus' death and resurrection, walking with the enabling power of Christ's spirit who is alive and seated at the right hand of God.

Ezra describes the joyful emotion of the repentant Babylonian captives, when they finished the temple's foundations. "When the builders laid the foundation of the temple of the Lord, the priests stood...and they sang responsively, praising and giving thanks to the Lord: For He is good, For His mercy endures forever toward Israel.

Then all the people shouted with a great shout, when they praised the Lord, because the foundation of the house was laid...But many of the... old men who had seen the first temple wept with a loud voice...." (Ezra 3:10-11). The young men were jubilant while the old men wept with joy to see the restoration of the temple's foundation, which was the benchmark of their recommitment to God. Likewise, Christians will be full of rejoicing when they are dwelling with the solid foundation of Christ's principles beneath them.

Rebuilding of the Walls

Another endeavor of the repentant Babylonian captives was to rebuild the walls of Jerusalem. Prior to the use of airplanes in times of war, cities fortified themselves with perimeter defense walls. These walls were designed to keep enemies from entering to plunder and burn the city.

According to the book of Nehemiah, virtually the entire population of the Jews joined in rebuilding the walls. The people included Priests, Levites, goldsmiths, perfumers and merchants. The wall was built with expediency, because "the people had a mind to work" (Nehemiah 4:6) and because it was essential to raise it quickly before the enemies could organize an attack. The threat of the adversary was so prevalent that Nehemiah instructed, "Those who built on the wall, and those who carried burdens, loaded themselves so that with one hand they worked at construction, and with the other they held a weapon" (Nehemiah 4:17).

As Christians, we must understand the need to "Be sober, be vigilant; because your adversary the devil walks about like a roaring lion, seeking whom he may devour"

(1 Peter 5:8). The Jews of old were faced with the threat of real warriors attacking them, to keep them from getting strong with fortified walls. The Apostle Paul said of New Testament Christians, "For we do not wrestle against flesh and blood, but against principalities, against powers, against the rulers of darkness of this age, against spiritual hosts of wickedness in the heavenly places. Therefore take up the whole armor of God, that you may be able to withstand in the evil day, and having done all, to stand" (Ephesians 6:12-13). The spiritual threat of Mystery Babylon is just as real today as the physical warriors were of yesterday. The Body of Christ must follow the repentant Babylonian captives' intensity of recognizing the enemy's threat and prepare themselves with the armor of God. The Apostle Peter said, "You also, as living stones, are being built up a spiritual house…that you may proclaim the praises of Him who called you out of darkness into His marvelous light" (1 Peter 2:5+9). Our weapons are not physical, but spiritual, as we draw close to God in righteousness, we find the favor of His grace and strength to withstand the rulers of darkness of this twenty first century.

Pagan Wives

While in Babylon for seventy years, the children of Israel mixed themselves in marriages with foreign women, contrary to their prophet's commands. This disobedience was devastating in the eyes of the leaders, who were seeking to restore Israel as a nation. The sight of the returning captives, along with their foreign wives and little children who could not even speak the language of Judah offended Nehemiah. He "Contended with them and cursed them, struck some of them and pulled out their hair, and made them swear by God saying, 'you shall not give your daughters as wives to their sons, nor take their daughters for your sons or yourselves'." Nehemiah went on to declare that this sin was the same that brought down Solomon, the wisest king in the history of the earth (Nehemiah 13:25-26). Nehemiah's passion was amazing, for no preacher or minister would get away with such antics today without being slapped with a lawsuit.

But Nehemiah's intensity over this issue causes one to wonder about the significance of this sin. Apparently the sin was so severe, that upon Ezra's praying, weeping and confessing before the public assembly of Jews concerning this breach, evoked this response. The people proclaimed, "We have trespassed against our God, and have taken pagan wives from the peoples of the land; yet now there is hope in Israel in spite of this. Now therefore let us make a covenant with our God to put away all these wives and those who have been born to them, according to the advice of my master and of those who tremble at the commandment of our God; and let it be done according to the law" (Ezra 10:2-3).

Can you imagine or grasp the magnitude of their repentance? They literally separated themselves from their own wives and children in obedience to God. No doubt, plenty of tears were shed in the days that followed. Ezra the priest commanded them, "You have transgressed and have taken pagan wives, adding to the guilt of Israel. Now therefore, make confession to the Lord God of your fathers, and do His will; separate yourselves from the peoples of the land, and from the pagan wives. Then all the assembly answered and said with a loud voice, 'Yes! As you have said, so we must do'" (Ezra 10:10-12). Today, Christians should never literally separate from a wife or children over doctrinal differences or because a family member is unsaved. However, we must understand the significance of the inspired Word's teaching regarding this Old Testament example and it's ramifications in the spiritual realm.

The prophets of the Lord understood the devastating affects of the Jews mixings their race with the pagans of the land of Canaan. Like oil and water, it will mix, but the result is the loss of effectiveness for the water to refresh or the oil to be fuel. The prophets commanded concerning Canaan, "The land which you are entering to possess is an unclean land, with the uncleanness of the peoples... with their abominations which have filled it from one end to another with their impurity. 'Now therefore... do not take their daughters to your sons; and never seek their peace or prosperity, that you may be strong and eat the good of the land, and leave it as an inheritance to your children forever'" (Ezra 9:11-12). Obedience to this command was preeminent to the spiritual health of the Jewish community and their survival as a nation.

When we as Christians choose to live the way the world lives, we enter a marriage of sorts: the blending of our lives with the lives of Mystery Babylon. In essence, we are seeking the prosperity that comes from the world's lifestyle, not from the faith and discipline of trusting God and His promises. When Christians make a lifestyle of behaving according to the norms of a pagan society, several things begin to happen. People respond to our testimony with sarcasm, "If that's what a Christian is, I don't want to be one." They understand that a Christian is supposed to be different. Secondly, we lose the life-giving principles of trusting God and because the principles are no longer evident in our daily life, they do not get passed on to our children. Soon, within a generation, our children are so blended with the world's ways, that they have lost any connection to the Christian life of faith, or "language of Judah". One aspect of the foundational doctrine of laying on of hands, is passing on to the next generation the values of God that we hold so dear.

No wonder the Apostle John was instructed to write of Mystery Babylon, "THE MOTHER OF HARLOTS AND THE ABOMINATIONS OF THE EARTH" (Revelation 17:5). For Christians to marry the covetous lifestyle of today's Mystery Babylon is to rob their children of Christian inheritance. Our disobedience will cause our children to have no concept of what it means to walk by faith or to trust the Lord. They will follow the Anti-Christ and his mark, just as their parents followed materialism to the exclusion of God and faithful attendance to church. We must recognize the severe consequences of disobedience and choose to repent and pursue God with all our hearts.

Jesus forewarned his disciples concerning the "day of the Lord." He said, "Take heed to yourselves, lest your hearts be weighed down with carousing, drunkenness, and cares of this life, and that Day come on you unexpectedly. For it will come as a snare on all those who dwell on the face of the whole earth. Watch therefore, and pray always that you may be counted worthy to escape all these things that will come to pass, and to stand before the Son of Man" (Luke 21:34-36). A snare is always hidden from sight. The snare of Mystery Babylon is man's pursuit of wealth, power and pleasure to the absence of God. In order to escape, we must follow the intense example of Ezra and Nehemiah in confessing our sins, repenting and returning to the precepts and judgments of the Lord. But what exactly is the worldliness that we are turning from?

According to the Apostle Paul, a covetous person will not inherit the kingdom of God (Ephesians 5:5). This is contrary to our society's present thinking. Because society views material gain as success, they delude themselves into believing their spiritual condition is okay if they are a good person. Jesus did not deny the rich young ruler had kept all the commandments from his youth up, yet he went away sorrowful when Jesus instructed him to sell all he had, give to the poor, and to come and follow Him. It was then that Jesus declared, "How hard it is for those who have riches to enter the kingdom of God!" (Mark 10:23). It is entirely possible to be a good person, work hard all your life and still end up condemned, because in the pursuit of a good life, they excluded God. As Christians, we are repenting from worldly lifestyles that seek to justify self with basic goodness and pursuit of material possessions, to the exclusion of God. This is the snare we are escaping from.

The Sabbath Day

In the prayer of confession recorded in Nehemiah chapter nine, the repentant Babylonian captives acknowledge their rebellion. They state, "You made known...Your holy Sabbath, and commanded them precepts, statutes and laws...but they and our fathers acted proudly, hardened their necks and did not heed Your commandments" (Nehemiah 9:14-16). Their response was to renew their commitment to the observance of the Sabbath day and the reading of God's laws. They made this solemn pledge, "We make a sure covenant and write it; Our leaders, our Levites and our Priest seal it... And enter into a curse and an oath to walk in God's Law, which was given by Moses the servant of

God, and to observe and do all the commandments of the
Lord...if the peoples of the land brought wares or any
grain to sell on the Sabbath day, we would not buy it
from them on the Sabbath...." (Nehemiah 9:38, 10:29-
31).

In today's Mystery Babylon, society thinks nothing of
conducting business and personal pleasure on the Sabbath
day. The world's behavior is understandable, for they
make no confession of following Christ. However,
Christians need to follow the example of the repentant
Babylonian captives and make priority each week for
attending the house of the Lord. Christians need to renew
their understanding of the day of rest and its value in
discovering a loving God who provides for their every
need.

God created Adam on the sixth day. Adam's first full
day of existence was the seventh day of creation. God
instructed Adam, that part of creation was to rest one day
in seven from his labors. Rest in the Hebrew is the word
shabath, pronounced shaw-bath. It is the root word for
Sabbath and conveys the idea of resting from labor for the
purpose of celebrating. Obviously, as Adam took his first
deep breaths of air and looked around at the New World
that was full of beauty, he had plenty of reason to
celebrate. His enlightened consciousness encompassed
the reality that God had created and provided everything.
God had designed the magnificence of every living thing
and he and Eve were created in God's image to share the
grandeur of life with the Father. As God walked and
talked with Adam on that seventh day, Adam discovered
the marvelous truth of the Sabbath day. He could have
chosen to immediately begin dressing the garden, but
instead he chose to spend time with the Creator,
celebrating creation and marveling at the undefiled world

before him. In return, he found the day was sanctified or separated and blessed. Adam experienced knowing God and being filled with the awe and wonder of the Creator's presence, with the assurance that God was his source for everything he needed in life.

The seventh day of creation is a continuing day of the creative process. God never instructed man to duplicate the second, third or fifth day of creation. However, He has repeatedly admonished man to remember the Sabbath, the seventh day of creation. It is the fourth of the Ten Commandments. Regardless of it's observance in paradise, before or after the fall of man, it's attention yields the same spiritual truth. When we spend one day in seven, resting from our labors to celebrate God, we are blessed. Blessed with the understanding that God is our provider and has made provision for everything we need. Blessed with understanding that life is about fellowship with God who instills within us hope, faith and expectation. As Creator, God imparts life to His creation. Whatever we need, He is the great "I Am" who is ever present to provide for us. Our resting from our labors and celebrating the Creator on the Sabbath, reminds us God has provided salvation for us even before our fall. The scriptures declare, "The Lamb slain from the foundation of the world" (Revelation 13:8). As we rest in the Lord, we realize we can not earn salvation with good works. We can only rest in His wonderful grace and marvel at His kindness, for God has provided even the salvation we need. If Adam needed to honor the Sabbath before the curse, how much more do we need to receive of its blessing after the curse?

With the same spirit of the repentant Babylonian captives, we need to return to the house of God and begin to honor the Sabbath. God does not receive any benefit by our attending, for God is complete within Himself. However, we receive the character of His spiritual life as the Creator imparts the knowledge of His precepts and wisdom to His creation. This weekly renewal transforms our fallen carnal nature into the image of Christ. Thereby we are enabled to become the person of faith who rises to the challenge "to him who overcomes," that Jesus repeatedly gave to the seven churches of Revelation, and receive the reward of sitting with Christ on His throne (Revelation 3:21).

Ezra, Nehemiah and the repentant Babylonian captives demonstrated broken and contrite hearts, in humbling themselves before God. This softness of heart toward the Lord is the basis of personal relationship. This relationship leads us into the realm of knowing God on an intimate level and all of His attributes of mighty power. This relationship with God has its beginnings in the creation story and leads us back to God's original purpose for man, to have dominion. This mighty power will enable Christians to overcome the mark of the Anti-Christ and instead trust Christ during the "hour of temptation," realizing that God is our source, not a clever politician who has control of the world's marketplace.

The Tithe

When the children of Israel came back from the Babylonian captivity, to rebuild Jerusalem, the people made a covenant among themselves under the leadership of Nehemiah, not to repeat the sins of their fathers. They determined to break the covetous spirit amongst themselves and restore the importance of the house of God to its rightful place. Ezra and Nehemiah's covenant reads, "Now the...people...entered into a curse and an oath to walk in God's Law, which was given by Moses...to observe and do all the commandments of the Lord...we would exact from ourselves...for the service of the house of God...we made ordinances to bring the firstfruits of our ground...to the house of the Lord...to bring the firstfruits of our dough, our offerings, the fruit from all kinds of trees... to the storerooms of the house of our God, to bring the tithes of our land to the Levites, for the Levites should receive the tithes in all our farming communities...and we will not neglect the house of our God" (Nehemiah 10:28-39). As Christians, we need to adopt the same heart attitude of repentance, to keep God's house as a place of importance in our lives and protect ourselves from being snared by Mystery Babylon.

A simple definition of covetousness in Mystery Babylon is to desires things, without godly restraint. Instead of waiting on God, the covetous pursue the possession with their wisdom and effort. Whenever I see a fancy Mercedes drive by, I can't help wondering if the owner is honoring the Lord with his tithes. If he is, then he is certainly enjoying the blessing of the Lord. If he is not honoring the Lord in giving, then he is a covetous man. If I were to use my tithes to buy a Mercedes, I could easily afford the payments. However, that would be using my own wisdom and effort, rather than waiting on the Lord for His provision and timetable for my life. The outward appearance would be one of success, but the inward reality would be a covetous spirit. I have a far greater need to build up my inner man, than to have my outward man appear prosperous. The quality of German engineering can not compare with the quality of God's character in the inner man.

The Prophet Malachi confronted his fellow Jews; "Will a man rob God? Yet you have robbed Me! But you say, 'in what way have we robbed You?' In tithes and offerings...Bring all the tithes into the storehouse, that there may be food in My house and try me now says the Lord of Host, if I will not open the windows of heaven and pour you out a blessing that there will not be room enough to receive it" (Malachi 3:8-10).

The history of God's chosen nation is a lesson in the carnal nature of the human heart. If anyone should have walked with God in gratefulness, it should have been the Jews. Unfortunately, it took the captivity of Babylon to shake Israel to her senses and realize the treasure of God's love and favor. Like the Hebrews of old, today it is the same statistical reality, the better the economy; the fewer people attend church. You would think people would want to attend church to thank God for His blessings. Instead, because life is so good, carnal men deceive themselves in to believing they don't really need God. The children of Israel went into the Babylonian captivity because of their covetousness. Mystery Babylon will ensnare the materialists of today for the same reason. If we are to be overcomers, we need to discipline ourselves to recognize the importance of giving faithfully our tithes to the house of the Lord each week as we come to celebrate the Creator.

People invest in insurance policies to protect themselves from disasters. Their consistent giving to the premiums assures them in the event of a catastrophe; they will be protected in their investment. As much as I despise insurance premiums, I must confess, those policies have saved me financially several times in car accidents, house fires and hurricane damage. Without the policy, I would have come to financial ruin.

Jesus shared a principle about money that insures spiritual prosperity. He said, "Do not lay up for yourselves treasures on earth, where moth and rust destroy and where thieves break in and steal; but lay up for yourselves treasures in heaven, where neither moth nor rust destroys and where thieves do not break in and steal. For where your treasure is, there your heart will be also" (Matthew 6:19-21). When we give to the house of the Lord, our hearts follow. We value wherever we invest our money.

The return on our investment in the house of the Lord, is a heart that is filled with spiritual strength, faith and patience as we grow in the knowledge of the Lord. God also pours out blessings from the windows of heaven, such that we can not receive it all, as we learn to obey Him in the tithe. This weekly experience of exchanging tithes and blessings brings the believer into the firm confidence that God is his source of material provision. And the consummate assurance that in the time of the mark of the Anti-Christ without which no one may buy or sell, God will provide for us in spite of the Anti-Christ's vehement proclamations to the contrary. Without the weekly exercise of honoring the Sabbath and tithing, we become weak in our faith and ultimately are sure to come to spiritual ruin.

The world would have us believe that we are independent when we prosper and do not need God. But the handiwork of creation communicates co-dependency. We need the oxygen the plants give in exchange for our exhaling carbon dioxide. The plant needs the insect that supplies the pollen to the ovum and the insect needs the plant for food. The man needs the woman, just as the woman needs the man. And man needs God for the spiritual character He gives, restoring us through Christ to the dominion for which man was created.

Consider what Jesus said, "For whoever desires to

save his life will lose it, but whoever loses his life for My sake will find it. For what will it profit a man if he gains the whole world, and loses his own soul? Or what shall a man give in exchange for his soul? For whoever is ashamed of Me and My words in this adulterous and sinful generation, of him the Son of Man also will be ashamed when He comes in the glory of His Father with the holy angels. Assuredly, I say to you, there are some standing here who shall not taste death till they see the Son of Man coming in His kingdom" (Matthew 16:25-28, Mark 8:35-38). A man demonstrates his shame of the Lord when he ignores attending faithfully the house of the Lord each week. He also declares his treasure each time he gives his money to everything but God's house. These simple acts speak louder than any affirmations to the contrary. To ignore God is to say, I am trying to gain more of the world with my own efforts. Jesus assures you, that if you could gain the whole world, it would still be possible for you to lose your soul, because you were not rich towards God.

Mystery Babylon is the embodiment of this scriptural truth. Men will reject God for the Anti-Christ's mark, giving them full access to the material wealth of the world. Choosing to pursue the world to gain life and materialism. Their faith and trust is in their own efforts and works. To them resting in the Lord means nothing.

But those who learn the simple principle of the seventh day of creation and honoring God with tithes, they are prepared to say no to the Anti-Christ's mark and believe that God is their source and provider. This preparation results from disciplining themselves to trust the Creator's provision for everything. He is more than able to sustain and gird them up with faith to endure future persecutions.

The Feast of Booths

As the Babylonian captives walked in repentance, they discovered and restored the feast of booths to their yearly activities. "And they found written in the Law...that the children of Israel should dwell in booths during the feast of the seventh month...so the whole assembly of those who had returned from the captivity made booths and sat under the booths; for since the days of Joshua the son of Nun until that day the children of Israel had not done so. And there was very great gladness" (Nehemiah 8:14-17). There are three major feasts in the annual calendar of Israel. They are known as the feasts of pilgrimage, for all Jewish males were required to travel to Jerusalem for these celebrations. These feasts have meaning and purpose that God desires to impart to His people. But the feast of Booths has special importance to New Testament Christians who will be enduring the persecutions of Mystery Babylon.

The first is the feast of Passover. Its observance reminded the Jews of God's protection from the death angel when the first born of Egypt were slain. The first born of Israel lived because of their obedience to slay a lamb without spot or blemish and to mark the doorpost and lintel of their house. The obvious application for Christians is the reality that Jesus was the lamb of God slain for us, so that if we believe in His shed blood, we are no longer first born, but born again and not subject to the angel of death.

The second is the feast of Weeks or Pentecost. It literally means fifty days and its application for the Jew is the remembrance of God's Law being given on Mount Sinai. For the Christian, we are reminded of its fulfillment fifty days after the resurrection of Jesus and the outpouring of the Holy Spirit. Jews follow the law, but Christians follow the Holy Spirit. It is the power of God's spirit that enables us to live victoriously. The third is the feast of Booths. The Jews were required to build small temporary huts and dwell in them for seven days to remind them of their wanderings in the wilderness forty years prior to their entering the Promised Land. There is a reason why Israel discontinued celebrating the feast during the days of Joshua's leading Israel into the promise land. The Jews felt they had arrived and there was no longer any need for such humility of being subjected to the elements of nature for seven days. However, great gladness came to them as they rediscovered the truths surrounding this feast in their repentance. Several truths can be seen in the feast of Booths. Each of these truths have magnificent promise for Christians who will endure Mystery Babylon, the time when saints will not be allowed to buy or sell because of their refusal to take the mark of the Anti-Christ. In a very real sense, we will be enduring a wilderness experience.

The celebration was also known as the feasts of tabernacles. Tabernacles refer to temporary dwelling places that the children of Israel were accustomed to during the wilderness experience of Exodus. Each time the glory cloud moved they packed up and followed. For all intents and purposes, Israel should have perished in the desert, but God sustained them. The repentant Babylonian captives realized the faithfulness of God once again to sustain them during their seventy years of bondage. For Christians, we need to realize God will not forsake us in Mystery Babylon, when we have no ability to buy or sell. After all, there were no grocery stores in the wilderness for the Jews to buy milk and eggs, yet God provided. The temporary booth was a reminder of Israel's exodus from Egypt, that they were pilgrims and strangers in the land. For Christians, as we walk in repentance towards God, we realize that Mystery Babylon is the spiritual desert of this world and that we are destined to go beyond this temporary earth to our heavenly mansions.

The celebration was also a reminder of the glory cloud that softened the heat of the blazing sun and the pillar of fire that gave them heat at night in the wilderness. Again, this is a reminder of the miraculous provision of God during times of trial. Christians will experience similar miraculous provisions during Mystery Babylon's persecutions.

Another ritual of the feast of Booths was erecting torches and lights to commemorate the Shekinah glory of God's presence coming on the Tabernacle of Moses during the wilderness journey.   Jesus said of Himself, "I am the light of the world," (John 8:12) and to His saints, "You are the light of the world" (Matthew 5:14). During this time in Mystery Babylon, our lights will shine forth in the midst of the shadow of the Anti-Christ. Christians will be shining examples of what it means to walk by faith, trusting in God and being filled with the Holy Spirit.

Surrounding the feast of Booths, was also the celebration of the ingathering of the harvest. The fall season was the time of gathering in the produce of the fields. The weeks of laboring were now being rewarded with the fruits of those labors. Correspondingly, during the time of Mystery Babylon, a great harvest of souls will be reaped as people recognize the truths of God's Word, and receive Christ as their Savior.

Just as God sustained Israel during ancient Babylon,

He will also sustain Christians during Mystery Babylon. We have a great need to seek God for His strength and character by repenting of our carnal ways, just as the repentant Babylonian captives did. For a great time of tribulation is coming to the earth and we need God's mercy and protection.

Daniel's Example

Throughout the scriptures, food has been used as an allegory to describe our spiritual nourishment. When Daniel came to Nebuchadnezzar's Babylon as a counselor, he was given a daily portion of the king's provisions. "But Daniel purposed in his heart that he would not defile himself with the portion of the king's delicacies, nor with the wine which he drank; therefore he requested of the chief of the eunuchs that he might not defile himself." The chief dietitian granted their request and after ten days of eating the prescribed meals, "Their features appeared better and fatter in flesh than all the young men who ate the portion of the king's delicacies" (Daniel 1:8+15). This story illustrates a wonderful spiritual truth. When Christians honor the Lord with obedience because of feeding on God's Word, their lifestyle and physical countenance will glow with the presence of the Lord. There is an obvious difference of physical appearance between Christians and those who feed on worldliness.

Jesus' Example

The Pharisee's asked when the kingdom of God would come, and Jesus replied, "The kingdom of God does not come with observation, ...for indeed, the kingdom of God is within you" (Luke 17:20-21). The deeds of men certainly reflect the kingdom of light and darkness. Solomon said, "Even a child is known by his deeds, whether what he does is pure and right" (Proverbs 20:11). Jesus confirmed this truth when He said, "Every good tree bears good fruit, but a bad tree bears bad fruit...therefore by their fruits you will know them" (Matthew 7:17+20). These latter days will purge the hearts of men, revealing the fruit of their souls. It will become obvious whether your heart loves the world or loves the Lord. It will also reveal the character of your soul, whether you have the faith and patience of the Lord.

As Christians, we walk in the example of the Lord. His example was in knowing He was the son of God and knowing He was sent from God for the purpose of the cross, laying down His life, suffering the persecution and rejection of men. He did it for the joy that was set before Him. In the same manner, we are instructed by the Lord, "He who does not take up his cross and follow Me is not worthy of Me. He who finds his life will lose it, and he who loses his life for My sake will find it" (Matthew 10:38-39). Each Christian should examine his own faith and ask himself the question, am I ready to suffer persecution, rejection and suffering for the Lord? The alternative to the cross is not very good. To reject Christ and pursue worldliness is fun for a season, as we seek to find fulfillment, but as Peter said, "All things will be dissolved, [therefore] what manner of persons ought you to be in holy conduct and godliness?" (2 Peter 3:11). This sobering reality should drive each of us to seek the Lord and to prepare our hearts with the character of strength to endure with patience those things, which are coming on the earth.

Ralph Waldo Emerson once said, "What lies behind us

and what lies before us are tiny matters compared to what lies within us." What lies within, is our Lord Jesus Christ. The Apostle John declared, "He who is in you is greater than he who is in the world" (1 John 4:4). The Lord's kingdom is like an acorn germinating the moment we are born again. Though it begins small, it eventually becomes a great oak, able to withstand the storms of life. Any kingdom starts out with a revolution and slowly grows in dominion. The Apostle Paul proclaimed, "My little children...I labor...until Christ be formed in you...." (Galatians 4:19). As we meditate on the principles of Christ, our countenance and spiritual strength are slowly transformed so that we are no longer like the world, but like Christ, able to endure persecution, rejection and suffering for the joy set before us.

When discussing character with my children, I tell them integrity is like the stars of night. That God is light and all of the specks of brightness are pinholes in the sky that reveal His nature. Likewise, all the little deeds of our lives reveal the brightness of God's character. Little things we do illuminate us as a star in His kingdom.

Get Out of Your Country

Abraham dwelt in Ur of the Chaldees. This city was located in Babylon under the dominion of Nimrod. God spoke to Abraham, "Get out of your country, from your family and from your father's house. To a land that I will show you. I will make of you a great nation; I will bless you and make your name great; and you shall be a blessing. I will bless those who bless you and I will curse him who curses you; and in you all the families of the earth shall be blessed" (Genesis 12:1-3).

Abraham's family and friends were of the mindset of

Nimrod's Babylonian persuasion. God wanted to bless Abraham, but in order to do so, Abraham had to separate himself from the wicked lifestyle of his native land. The Babylonians were saying, "Let us build us a city, and a tower whose top is in the heavens; let us make a name for ourselves, lest we be scattered abroad over the face of the whole earth" (Genesis 11:4). Upon close examination, God was offering Abraham in exchange for his obedience, the same thing the Babylonians were seeking to achieve with their own efforts. Abraham believed God and it was accounted to him for righteousness and he was brought to the Promised Land.

As children of Abraham, we believe in Jesus Christ and it is likewise accounted to us for righteousness. We are challenged in these latter days with the same admonition, get out of Mystery Babylon (Revelation 18:4). As Christians we need to put off the ways of the world and pursue a godly relationship with Christ in attending church and learning to honor God with our tithes and offerings. As we obey, God's hand will be with us every step of the way. Through faith, God will lead and guide us, protecting us from our enemies as He brings us to "The city which has foundations, whose builder and maker is God" (Hebrews 11:10).

Chapter 13

How Christians Will Survive!
"The Schindler Principle"

"Because you have kept My command to persevere, I also will keep you from the hour of trial which shall come upon the whole world, to test those who dwell on the earth." Revelation 3:10

The prophecies of Jeremiah concerning Israel and the impending Babylonian captivity began coming to pass. Nebuchadnezzar and the Babylonians (Chaldeans) were building siege mounds against the walls of Jerusalem. Jeremiah assured the Israelites that God would not forsake them forever, but the day would come when they would inhabit the land once again. In the context of Israel's certain demise, while Jeremiah was in prison for his pessimistic prophecies, God instructed the jailed prophet to buy a piece of land from his cousin. The land purchase in the midst of the military distress was a sign that God would eventually bring Israel back to their inheritance. The prophet declared, "There is nothing too hard for You [God]." And the word of the Lord came to Jeremiah, "Behold, I am the Lord, the God of all flesh. Is there anything to hard for Me?" (Jeremiah 32:17+26). God was assuring His people of His watchful protection during their captivity and of their ultimate return. In the same way, God wants the saints to understand He will not forsake them during the time of the Anti-Christ, but will provide for them until the coming of the "day of the Lord." For with God, nothing is too hard!

Daniel, Shadrach, Meshach and Abednego lived under pagan kings, in a pagan land during the Babylonian captivity. Through wisdom, they learned to cooperate with ungodly authority and not to compromise their godly convictions. Although the hour of testing, (being required to worship Nebuchadnezzar's golden image) came upon the known world of their time, they survived because of the protection of God's hand. Likewise, the Anti-Christ of Mystery Babylon will require the world to worship his image and take the mark in order to buy and sell. Nevertheless, Christians will find God's protection during the hour of testing that will come upon the whole world.

Jesus assured the church of Philadelphia, He would keep them from the "hour of trial" that is coming (Revelation 3:10). Like the Hebrew children of the book of Daniel, because of their faithfulness and perseverance, God will provide for the faithful with His sovereign hand. Christians who trust God during this time will come to know what Daniel meant when he wrote of the latter days, "The people who know their God shall be strong, and carry out great exploits" (Daniel 11:32). Just because the Anti-Christ controls the ability to buy and sell, does not make null and void the pledge of God to provide for His saints. God is still the one who promised, "Therefore do not worry, saying 'what shall we eat?' or 'what shall we drink?' or 'what shall we wear?' ...for your heavenly Father knows that you need all these things. But seek first the kingdom of God and His righteousness, and all these things will be added to you" (Matthew 6:31-33). Here are several ways throughout history that God has provided for His people during tribulation.

The Supernatural

Throughout the history of Israel, God has used the

miraculous to provide for His people. During the time of wandering in the wilderness, God gave manna from heaven to sustain the Israelites. The frost-like substance which fell like dew, was a statement of the faithfulness that God would never leave nor forsake them.

Another act of miracle provision was given to Elijah, while fleeing from the corrupt government of Ahab and Jezebel. The king and queen had ordered Elijah's execution and he was on the run. God instructed Elijah to go eastward and dwell by a brook, where ravens came and fed him with bread and meat, while he drank from the brook. Once the brook dried up from the drought, God had another provision in place for sustaining the righteous prophet.

When the multitudes grew weary, Jesus fed them miraculously by multiplying the loaves and fish. When confronted with paying taxes, Jesus instructed Peter to cast a fishing hook and bring in a fish and the tax money would be in the fish's mouth.

Missionaries on foreign fields have frequently shared their experiences of supernatural provision when they found themselves in difficult and extreme circumstances. Testimonies of the poor within our churches declare the glory of God's providential grace in times of their needs. When Christians are confronted with the perplexing reality of not being able to buy or sell in Mystery Babylon, they will find God moving on their behalf in many extraordinary ways. God will use the supernatural to care for the saints.

The Favor of the World

Another tool God uses is giving saints favor in the eyes of the world. When the Israelites were leaving

Egypt, God moved on the hearts of the Egyptians to bless them with provisions. "Let every man ask from his neighbor and every woman from her neighbor, articles of silver and articles of gold. And the Lord gave the people favor in the sight of the Egyptians" (Exodus 11:2-3). That favor was used by God to provide for their journey into the wilderness.

When the two spies entered Jericho to spy out the land, Rahab the harlot hid them. Her kindness spared their lives and was remembered by God. She helped them because she discerned the Israelites were truly God's people. She declared, "For the Lord your God, He is God in heaven above and on the earth beneath!" (Joshua 2:11). She understood the larger picture, though Jericho was the greatest of the cities of Canaan, God's will was greater.

During the time of the Anti-Christ, there will be many people who don't believe the Anti-Christ is God. But they will still bow with disingenuous reverence towards his image in order to maintain the privilege of buying and selling. Many of these people will see the injustice of the Anti-Christ towards Christians and will seek to be a blessing, sustaining the Christians with provisions.

When Elijah was fleeing from the execution orders of Ahab and Jezebel, God spoke to him, "Arise and go to Zarephath, which belongs to Sidon, and dwell there. See, I have commanded a widow there to provide for you." When Elijah requested a little water to drink and a morsel of bread to eat, she replied. "As the Lord your God lives, I do not have bread, only a handful of flour in a bin, and a little oil in a jar; and see, I am gathering a couple of sticks that I may go in and prepare it for myself and my son, that we may eat and die" (1 Kings 17:9-16). Ironically, Elijah instructed her to prepare the food for him to eat first and then for her family, attaching a promise that God would provide for her until the rains came again. God provided for Elijah, through the graciousness of a Gentile widow.

One of the realities of the Roman persecution in the first century, is that many chose to burn incense to the Emperor as a god to avoid oppression. It was purely a decision to avoid confrontation on their part and their hearts were never sincere in worship. History records that many of these same people aided the persecuted Christians by hiding them or giving them food and essentials for living. Many of the Christians in Rome hid in the catacombs and would come out under the cover of darkness to receive the gifts of those who helped them.

After the holocaust of Nazi Germany, many stories surfaced as survivors shared the kindness shown to them by those who disagreed with the political view of Hitler's government. *The Diary of Anne Frank* and the testimony of Corrie Ten Boom are but the tip of the iceberg, of those who were moved with compassion to sustain the Jews in their hour of need. God moved upon the hearts of those who were sensitive, to the point of risking punishment and retribution for serving the Jews who were being singled out for the "SS" concentration camps.

Even today, missionaries who work in the underground church of China report of the compassion of those who seek to guard and protect those preaching the gospel. A network of trusted friends allow itinerate Chinese preachers to flee from the government and keep moving to avoid capture. During the time of the Anti-Christ, God will raise up many individuals to minister to the saints, sustaining and providing for their necessities.

Fruit of the Land

In my travels, I have been in several third world countries visiting with pastors in remote areas and villages. I have often observed primitive conditions of people who live without running water, electricity and no grocery store for many miles. I have often thought to myself, the concerns of these people are what stream they will fish and what banana tree they will climb tomorrow. They usually have chickens, pigs, cows and a crop growing in the field behind their shack. Multitudes in third world countries live this way everyday. It is possible!

To this day, one of my greatest experiences as a Christian was dwelling among a community of believers in a remote rural grassland in Central America. The fellowship of the native brethren was a sweet reminder of what the body of Christ is meant to be. The people helped one another to survive, living off the land. The days were filled with hard work in managing the animals and crops. In the evenings after dinner, the people would gather to worship Jesus Christ, share the knowledge of the scriptures and fellowship with one another. The hut I stayed in had a dirt floor with open windows that could be closed in bad weather. The doors were always open during the day and visited frequently by the live stock. There was an outhouse for bathing, utilizing a bucket and sponge and an outhouse for sanitary purposes. I asked one young person who had returned from Los Angeles, why she would come back to live here after enjoying modern conveniences. The reply was centered on the love, warmth and affection of her immediate and extended Christian family. Something that no amount of materialism, entertainment or finances could possibly replace. She had found Christ and the unique glow of her Christian community was more fulfilling than the love of the world.

A fond conversation reminds me of this primitive way of living. The premise of this book was being discussed with a missionary friend of mine who serves in the remote mountain villages of Bolivia. My friend laughed at the thought of the Anti-Christ's mark and said, "He'll have a tough time implementing the mark on the mountain where I live. My folks don't buy and sell; they don't have any money. They bring potatoes, beans and eggs for the offering plate."

I remember in my early childhood years, the farmhouse of my grandparents in the mountains of Virginia. I still remember bringing pails of fresh spring water into the kitchen to drink and the outhouse down the trail that everyone loathed to use after nightfall because the batteries were dead in the flashlight. I recall the firewood stacked near the door that was used for the wood stoves. I remember granny sending us to get eggs from the hen house, her cooking on a wood cook stove and the cellar where they kept potatoes, jars of green beans and canned apples. I remember the garden where granddad planted the corn and prayed for rain to bless the harvest. It wasn't that long ago that many Americans lived the same way foreigners live in third world countries today.

During the Roman persecution, many Christians simply moved to the hills and carved out an existent for themselves in the country. This is exactly what David did when King Saul was seeking after him. He hid himself in the mountains and countryside. Granted, times were extremely tough as they were for my grandparents and all who have experienced living off the land. But it is possible! When the Israelites entered the promise land, the manna ceased because the fruit of the land was great enough to sustain them. Living off the land will certainly be one alternative that God will use to provide for some.

Jesus told the story of the unjust steward to illustrate a truth to his followers. The unjust steward discovered that he was soon to be released from the employment of his master. Because he was physically unable to dig and despised the thought of begging, he took the bills of his master's debtors and cut them in half to build friendship with them. So that upon his release, they would receive him into their houses as friends. Jesus declared, "The master commended the unjust steward because he had dealt shrewdly. For the sons of this world are more shrewd in their generation than the sons of light. And I say to you, make friends for yourselves by unrighteous mammon, that when you fail, they may receive you into an everlasting home" (Luke 16:8-9).

A constructive way for Christians to observe this scripture is to consider giving liberally to the mission field. In a sense, you are canceling men's debts before God by underwriting their souls being won to the Lord with the gospel via missionaries. Our missionaries are doing tremendous works of righteousness and building goodwill with people in the uttermost parts of the earth. Those people are in turn grateful to those who helped them with the knowledge of salvation. Thus you have built friendships with those who know how to live off the land and you may one day have to call upon them for assistance, to flee from the persecution of the Anti-Christ in metropolitan areas.

As these last days develop prior to the implementing of the Anti-Christ's mark and men discern the wisdom of this simple investment, the gospel will be strengthened in going to the uttermost parts of the earth. This will fulfill the pre-requisite of the Lord, "And this gospel of the kingdom will be preached in all the world as a witness to all the nations, and then the end will come." Certainly those who "flee to the mountains" will help carry and promote the gospel message (Matthew 24:14+16). In that day and hour, they will be asked by third world natives, why they have left the comforts of the modern world to come to live among the poorest of society. The answer will be simple. There no longer remains anything among the rich for the fleeing Christian.

Peter asked a question of Jesus, "We have left all and followed You. Therefore what shall we have?" Jesus said, "Everyone who has left houses or brothers or sisters or fathers or mothers or wife or children or lands, for My name's sake, shall receive a hundredfold, and inherit eternal life. But many who are first will be last, and the last first" (Matthew 19:27-30). Receiving a hundredfold could very well apply to all the friends you have built up from investing in the mission field. The third world poor are looked upon by the world as last, but suddenly they become first in the eyes of God and Christians seeking refuge among them.

The Favor of Businessmen

Stephen Spielberg's movie "Schindler's List" was a moving depiction of a businessman who employed Jews during the holocaust of Nazi Germany in order to provide for and save them. His motive at first was one of greed that turned to compassion. His example will be duplicated many times over in the last days of the Anti-Christ's Mystery Babylon. I call this the Schindler Principle.

If you are an excellent employee with solid work habits, employers will still seek after you during the time of the mark of the beast. Granted, there will be enormous changes in how you are reimbursed for your work. If you can not buy and sell, there will be no need for health insurance, a retirement pension, bonuses, dental plans, a paycheck or automatic deposits. But this is precisely the key that motivates the employer to retain your services. He still needs crafts and skilled workers to make wealth and if you are the talent he is contented with, then the employer will find a way to accommodate your predicament. After all, if you have not taken the mark then the government doesn't know you exist and he will not have to pay employment taxes, FICA, social security, workman's compensation and a host of other government regulations. Shrewd businessmen know how to make wealth and when they see an opportunity to capitalize, they will. They may have to provide you with shelter, food and clothing in a variety of creative ways, but this is minimal compared to paying competitive wages. Employers have been working illegal immigrants for years. How much more will they be willing to help a conscientious worker who's only sin is objection to taking the mark of the beast and worshipping his image? They will view it as an occasion to make wealth, as well as show kindness to a good and faithful employee who has been loyal down through the years.

Christians will come to realize work is not a curse, but a blessing. God instructed Adam to dress the garden before the fall. Work is an opportunity to serve God and receive God's blessings in return. Work is rendering to God, the gift He has given to you, but belongs to God. If Christians can continue working discreetly for an employer, it will be much better than constantly running and hiding the reality that you cannot participate in the economy and are idle with your time. So whatever situation one finds themselves in during this persecution, Christians will continue to work and honor the Lord with their gifts and talents.

Opportunities may be as simple as being a house servant who cares for the home or a nanny who cares for the children while the master is at work in exchange for room and board. Perhaps you will be the grounds keeper or gardener. Or maybe you will continue to go to the office and maintain your area of responsibility in exchange for modest meals, shelter and transportation. You may continue your present employment responsibilities in exchange for provision through barter. Mediums of exchange will be numerous, as Christians and business people work out the details of their relationship. Obviously, as the time of the implementation of the mark for buying and selling approaches, Christians will need to quietly and discretely gain the trust of their employers. They will need to share their decision not to take the mark and inquire of the possibilities of an alternative employment arrangement. It will be important to exercise the utmost care and discernment, for one small breach of confidence could result in the Christian being turned over to the Anti-Christ.

Corporate Entities

For all intents and purposes, a corporation is considered an entity as much as an individual. The reason for incorporation of a business or any other organization is to transfer liability separate from the individual to the corporation. Thus, the corporation becomes recognized as a separate entity. Obviously, corporations buy and sell and do not have a hand in which to implant a mark. It may be possible for Christians to survive during the persecution by hiding behind the legalese of a corporation.

Sharp lawyers, who have a compassionate heart may find legal loop holes for Christians to utilize. So that all buying and selling is done through the camouflage of the legal entity of incorporation, without taking the mark in your right hand or forehead. The scriptures declare, "No one may buy or sell except one who has the mark or the name of the beast, or the number of his name" (Revelations 13:17). A corporation may be able to buy and sell with only the name or number of the Anti-Christ.

Consideration must be done with extreme conscientious consideration. Christians must remember the reason why they are refusing to take the mark of the beast. Christians will not worship the Anti-Christ as God, because it violates their conscience toward God and because taking the mark according to the Apostle John, is the same as forfeiting their opportunity for salvation (Revelation 14:9-11). Hiding behind a corporate charter with the motive of getting access to an alternative way of buying and selling may mean those who incorporated are worshippers of the Anti-Christ as God. It is important that God knows the attitude of their heart. This is why the hour of testing is coming on the whole world. Each Christian will have to carefully discern his motive and the wording of the corporate charters before using them to buy and sell.

However God chooses, there will be ample opportunities for Christians to discover ways to survive the persecution of the Anti-Christ without the personal ability to buy and sell. All over the world, Christians will be walking in the reality of the scriptures, "The just shall live by faith" (Hebrews 10:38). God will move on the hearts of men to facilitate the believers. The witness of saints enduring hardships because of their reverence for Jesus Christ will be a powerful tool that God will use to speak into the hearts of non-believers. The ability to be content in the simplicity of Christ, living without covetousness will certainly be a statement of pious living. This Godly character will be an admonishment to a world that believes wealth and materialism is the goal of life. God is going to judge mankind for taking the mark and worshipping the Anti-Christ. God may very well point to the persecuted Christian's simple lifestyle, as evidence against all who justified themselves with the excuse, well what was I suppose to do, I had to eat!

Chapter 14

The Babylonish Garment!
"The Achan Lad"

"These are the statutes and judgments which you shall be careful to observe in the land which the Lord God of your fathers is giving you to possess, all the days that you live on the earth...you shall seek the place where the Lord your God chooses...to put His name for His dwelling place; and there...you shall take your offerings, your tithes...." Dueteronomy 12:1+5-6

As the nation of Israel was coming out of bondage from Egypt, and from its wandering in the wilderness forty years, they began possessing the land of Canaan. The first task given to them by God was to march around Jericho seven days. And at the blowing of the trumpet, they were to cross over the collapsed walls, burn the city and gather the silver, gold, bronze and iron and put it in the treasury of the house of the Lord. Their conquering of Canaan came to an abrupt halt when it was discovered that one of the Israelites named Achan had broken the covenant by stealing the goods that were earmarked for the treasury of the house of the Lord. This story and their possessing the Promised Land are parallel to the last day's saints possessing the promises of God. Dwelling in the promises of God certainly requires us to fight the giants of the carnality, warring against the lusts of the flesh and maintaining the lordship of Christ as preeminent in our lives. We must constantly guard ourselves from the spirit of covetousness and the lifestyle of worldliness, lest we find ourselves being powerless to live the promises of God and to possess the Promised Land.

Promise Land Instructions

The book of Joshua records God's instructions to the children of Israel regarding the first fruits of possessing Canaan. "By all means, abstain from the accursed things, lest you become accursed when you take from the accursed things, and make the camp of Israel a curse and trouble it. But all the silver and gold...are consecrated to the Lord; they shall come into the treasury of the Lord" (Joshua 6:18-19). God was telling the Israelites to honor Him by offering the first fruits of Jericho to the Lord. This first fruits offering was in keeping with the commandments of the law and its observance communicated to God, His rightful position of first place in our lives.

Each Christian must learn to honor the Lord with tithes. Offerings are an act of worship that remind us of God's salvation, that He brought us out of Egypt and from wandering in the wilderness. Our disciplined obedience in tithes strengthens the treasury of the house of the Lord and allows God's ministry to invest on our behalf. Those personal tithes ultimately proclaim His name and wonderful works before mankind, acknowledging the greatness of our savior. They also teach us that God is our source and not money. Thus strengthening our faith towards God.

It is for this reason that God warns us in the New Testament not to get caught up in worldliness. "Do not love the world or the things in the world. If anyone loves the world, the love of the Father is not in him. For all that is in the world-the lust of the eyes, and the pride of life-is not of the Father but is of the world. And the world is passing away, and the lust of it; but he who does the will of God abides forever" (1 John 2:15-17). When God sees someone who is caught up in materialism to the point of casting aside his worshipful duty of tithing, God knows that He is no longer first place in the individual's life. Though God loves the individual very much, his worldliness communicates to the Father, "the love of, or for the Father" is not in him. The honest truth is, most people's checkbooks speak loud and clear in their testimony of gratefulness for the Lord's salvation, for good or bad.

The Apostle James admonishes, "You lust and do not have. You covet and cannot obtain...You ask and do not receive, because you ask amiss, that you may spend it on your pleasures. Adulterers and adulteresses! Do you not know that friendship with the world is enmity with God? Whoever therefore wants to be a friend of the world makes himself an enemy of God. Or do you think that the Scripture says in vain, 'The Spirit who dwells in us yearns jealously'"? (James 4:2-5). God is harshly condemning covetousness, because He knows the covetous spirit ultimately leads us away from the joy of the Lord and into bed with the great harlot Mystery Babylon (Revelation 17:5). God is a jealous God! He longs for us to know Him and to protect us from other lovers who will seek to destroy us. Certainly, Mystery Babylon and the Anti-Christ will seek our destruction, therefore we must listen carefully to the heart of God as He teaches us from the example of Joshua leading the Israelites into the Promised Land.

The Broken Covenant

Joshua records a triumphant entry into Jericho, which was the largest city of the land of Canaan. The Jews were basically powerless to overtake the city on their own;

instead it was the mighty hand of God who was
upholding them. Unknown to Joshua, a Jew named
Achan brought the curse of the Lord upon Israel because
he took of the accursed thing. Joshua did not discover
this until a few thousand Israelites lost the next battle to
the small town of Ai. This set back put Joshua into a
panic, seeking God for an answer because the broken
covenant had enormous ramifications. Joshua's prayers
acknowledged the danger of the Amorites destroying
Israel, of the Jews themselves being weakened in heart
and growing cowardice in their ability to stand before the
enemy, along with the name of the Jews and of God being
diminished (Joshua 7:7-9).

What Achan did may seem very harmless in the eyes
of many, but his sin struck at the heart of our individual
relationship with God and has equally devastating
consequences to every believer. Upon investigation, it
was discovered that Achan had transgressed God's
covenant by stealing of the silver and gold, deceiving the
others and putting it among his own stuff. When Joshua
inquired of the sin, Achan confessed, "When I saw
among the spoils a beautiful Babylonian garment, two
hundred shekels of silver, and a wedge of gold...I coveted
them and took them. And there they are, hidden in ...the
midst of my tent" (Joshua 7:20-21).

Garments throughout the scriptures have meaning.
Joseph's coat of many colors reflected the favor of his
father towards his son. David's rejection of Saul's armor
for his shepherd's clothing when slaying Goliath reflected
his distrust of man's invention and his confidence in the
Lord. The Babylonish garment revealed the heart of
Achan, demonstrating he was very materialistic and his
trust was in possessing wealth, not in the Lord. The
garment represented the worldly lifestyle of the

Babylonians, which had been slated for destruction by God, but Achan's desire for it demonstrated his priority of trusting wealth before trusting the Lord. It was very self centered, "I saw, I coveted, I stole, I hid, in my tent!"

The Babylonish garment was a reflection of Achan's love for the world, manifesting itself in breaking covenant with God. How? By taking of the silver and gold that rightfully belonged in the treasury of the house of the Lord and instead putting the wealth in the midst of his own tent and among his own stuff. What about us...do we follow Achan by robbing God of our offerings or do we truly believe He is our savior and honor Him with tithes? Most people tell me they can't afford to give tithes. What they mean is their budget is already so tight; they don't have enough money left over after each paycheck to give ten percent to God. The answer is simple. Take off the Babylonish garment by lowering your standard of living ten percent. Give to the treasury of the house of God what is rightfully His. Sell that big house, move into a smaller one and lower the mortgage. Trade in the new car for a used one with a smaller monthly payment. Stop eating out in restaurants so frequently and carefully choose the groceries each week by learning to do without those name brands and eating generic brands.

The response I get from many is, I can't do that! Why not, where is their gratefulness to God for His salvation? They probably spent the same amount of money on cigarettes and alcohol before they got saved. Many have been delivered from expensive drug habits or therapy sessions and yet now they can't seem to honor God with the money saved as a result of His deliverance. The truth is, people are very prideful and conscientious of the world, therefore they put on the Babylonish garment.

They put the silver and gold that belongs to the treasury of the house of God among their own stuff, in the midst of their own tent, so they can keep up with the Jones.

The Consequences

The possession of Canaan came to a halt! In order for them to move on, the Israelites were required to come into an agreement with God about Achan's sin. The judgment was pronounced, "Because he has done a disgraceful thing in Israel... then Joshua and all Israel with him, took Achan ...the silver, the garment, the wedge of gold, his sons, his daughters...and all that he had, and brought them to the Valley of Achor... So all Israel stoned him with stones; and they burned them with fire...then they raised over him a great heap of stones...and the name of that place has been called the Valley of Achor to this day" (Joshua 7:15+24-26).

This seems extremely harsh. But God's lessons are written as reminders to keep us in His love and protection. The spirit of worldliness brings us to a weakened character, where we cowardly submit to the enemy. In Mystery Babylon, if we don't have the strength to overcome the love of money and materialism, then we will surely take the mark of the beast and lose our opportunity for salvation, just as Achan lost his inheritance in the promise land. The name of the Lord and our personal reputations are diminished when we demonstrate to the world that we are no different from them. We are supposed to live by faith, not by a paycheck! In the end, we will cowardly submit to the Anti-Christ's persuasion and seek to justify ourselves. Our failure to honor God in offerings weakens the ministry's ability to promote the name of the Lord and strengthens the enemy's message of opulence.

Achan's family suffered the same capital punishment as he did! One may reason, if the "day of the Lord" is going to tarry for several more decades, it won't affect me. But our Babylonish lifestyle affects our children. How will they be able to withstand Satan if they see our example as being one of placing little significance on the house of the Lord? They will grow up following our example, like seed producing like seed. For the sake of our reputations, the name of the Lord and our children's sake, we must by example teach our children to honor God and faithfully obey His Word.

The heap of stones was a constant reminder to the Israelites of the covenant transgression that took place. Each time a Jew passed by, he was reminded of the lesson of covetousness. Achor is a version of Achan's name and it means trouble. The Valley of Achor became a symbol throughout the scriptures that was used by the prophets as a historical visual aid to teach the nation of Israel the dangers of covetousness. The prophets of old forewarned of the Babylonian captivity, if Israel failed to repent of covetousness. The fate of Mystery Babylon and the Anti-Christ's mark awaits all that seduce themselves with the lust for materialism. Achan was burned with fire and the judgment of Mystery Babylon is brimstone as well.

The Apostle Paul wrote of his concern about covetousness. He said, "Be imitators of God...and walk in love, as Christ has given Himself for us, an offering and a sacrifice to God, a sweet-smelling aroma. But ...covetousness, let it not even be named among you, as is fitting for saints...for this you know, that no ...covetous man ...has any inheritance in the kingdom of Christ and God. Let no one deceive you with empty words, for because of these things the wrath of God comes upon the sons of disobedience" (Ephesians 5:1-6).   Paul is challenging Christians to awaken from their slumber and make Christ Lord in this area of their lives. God did not call us to salvation from all manner of evil, only to see us lose our inheritance because we became basically good people who loved materialism more than the church. God is calling His people to repentance.

What Could Have Been

There is a strange aspect of Achan that deserves observation. All of his family members were godly men. Each of their names reflects the godly characteristics of Achan's ancestors. Jewish names always meant something and they were given as a reflection of the individual or times.

Achan's tribe was Judah and Judah means praise. Achan was from the Zarhites and his great grandfather was Zerah.   The name means to radiate light like the rising of the sun. His grandfather's name was Zabdi and means a spirit of giving, to confer upon others in giving gifts.   His father's name was Carmi. The name Carmi means to be a gardener, as in raising vineyards.   These names of the ancestry suggest a very solid, Godly upbringing for Achan. He had a long history of being taught to radiate the light of the Lord, to imitate God in the spirit of giving, to be fruitful, producing the spirit of the Lord in all he did. But for some reason, Carmi's son was named Achan, which means trouble, as when peaceful water is disturbed.   Achan's spirit and countenance was one of rebellion and the father knew it. Despite godly upbringing, he was determined to do things his way and eventually brought trouble to himself and his household.

Israel dealt with the sin of covetousness and moved on conquering Canaan, receiving their inheritance. Achan was burned and left behind. It was never God's plan, nor the desire of his relatives, but it happened as a result of Achan's personal choice. Oddly, the generation before him was left to wander in the wilderness until they died, because of unbelief. Achan's generation was raised up to be a witness of people who walked with God by faith, believing and trusting to overcome every giant in the Promised Land. They were born and called to be the generation of conquerors that witnessed the mighty power and demonstrations of the Lord, helping them to slay the giants of Anakim. God gave them a mighty calling and purpose.

God's Mighty Army

God never destines anyone to be like Achan, who defaulted on a great and mighty purpose in life, by succumbing to the spirit of worldliness. Each generation has its destiny rooted in the plan of God. The Lord declares that we are His creation, known of God before the foundation of the world. We are created for His purposes! Consider the words of David, "I will praise You, for I am fearfully and wonderfully made, marvelous are Your works, and that my soul knows very well. My frame was not hidden from You, when I was made in secret, and skillfully wrought in the lowest parts of the earth. Your eyes saw my substance, being yet unformed. And in Your book they all were written, **the days fashioned for me**, when as yet there were none of them. How precious also are Your thoughts to me, O God! How great is the sum of them! If I should count them, they would be more in number than the sand...." (Psalm

139:14-18).

Our generation *is destined* for this hour. God created us to be His latter day warriors, who slay every giant of covetousness in the Promised Land of dwelling with God. *These last days were fashioned for our generation*, to demonstrate to the world a better way of living. Mystery Babylon with all of her materialistic possessions and the Anti-Christ with his mark, is not our source of sustenance. Instead, our Lord Jesus Christ who is "The same yesterday, today and forever" declared to us, "Let your conversations be without covetousness; be content with such things as you have. For...I will never leave nor forsake you. So we may boldly say: The Lord is my helper, I will not fear. What can man do to me?" (Hebrews 13:8+5-6).   God's meditations toward us are thoughts of faith and strength. He looks knows we have the patience to endure and longs for us to trust Him in these hours of temptation. He sees us as we were before the creation of the earth, prepared for this generation, to proclaim His glory, exalt His name and to reign victorious over the Anti-Christ by drawing on His strength.

Jesus' name is identical to the Old Testament name of Joshua in meaning and purpose.   Just as Joshua led the Israelites to victory in Canaan, so Jesus leads us to triumph in the land of God's promises, dwelling with God according to His promises. "Thanks be to God who gives us the victory through our Lord Jesus Christ!"   (1 Corinthians 15:57).

Chapter 15

Conclusion
"Victory through the Mind of Christ"

*"Let this mind be in you which was also in Christ Jesus,
who humbled Himself and became obedient to the point
of death, even the death of the cross...for it is God who
works in you both to will and to do for His good
pleasure...that you may become blameless and harmless,
children of God without fault in the midst of a crooked
and perverse generation, among whom you shine as
lights in the world...."*
Philippians 2:5+8+13+15

During a shopping excursion, my children wanted to
go to the dollar store to buy some Christmas gifts. On
previous occasions we had often found some great deals
there. On this particular day we discovered snow globes
marked down to a buck. These globes were beautiful,
inside the glass dome was the nativity scene depicting
Joseph and Mary, the baby Jesus and the jubilant
shepherds. The base and figures inside the globe were
painted gold. When you shook the globe, little white
flakes fell simulating a white Christmas. It seemed to be
the perfect gift for only one dollar, until we wound up the
key and played the music. The Christmas carol was not
"Oh Little Town of Bethlehem" as labeled, instead it
played "Frosty the Snow Man."

When Jesus talked about His coming, it was in
response to the disciples exulting over the beauty of the
temple. Jesus wanted His disciples to understand the
kingdom of God had nothing to do with beautiful

architecture or the material value of a temple. The scripture reads, "Then, as some spoke of the temple, how it was adorned with beautiful stones and donations, He said, these things which you see-the days will come in which not one stone shall be left upon another that shall not be thrown down" (Luke 21:5-6). Just as the Roman empire destroyed the temple in 70 AD and took apart the stones to recover the melted gold that seeped into the mortar joints, God will destroy all that we see during the "day of the Lord." The only thing remaining of the kingdom will be that which is spirit, for "God is spirit." The Apostle Peter describing "the day of the Lord," said of this moment, "The genuineness of your faith, being much more precious than gold that perishes, though it is tested by fire, may be found to praise, honor, and glory at the revelation of Jesus Christ" (1 Peter 1:7). The Apostle Paul said, "Your body is the temple of the Holy Spirit, who is in you...." (1 Corinthians 6:19). What remains after "the day of the Lord" is the character of the Lord we received, because we faithfully pursued the Lord during our earthly walk.

The trial of our faith is going to be tested in the coming years by mocking men who say, "where is the promise of His coming" and the temptation of the covetousness of Mystery Babylon. As society begins to find its solution to governing the burgeoning masses with the universal personal identification code, increasing pressure will come upon Christians to conform to the world economic system. As the Anti-Christ is revealed, peer pressure will turn to persecution. Christians will need to call upon the Lord's Spirit, as they exercise faith and patience in choosing to forfeit the ability to buy and sell, as the mark of the beast is finally implemented. As we choose to take up our cross daily, our faith and patience will be developed each step of the way as the signs of the time progress.

When asked by Jesus, "Who do you say I am," Peter answered from divine inspiration, "You are the Christ, the Son of the living God." Once the disciples had grasped the revelation by which the church would be built upon, the scriptures say, "From that time Jesus began to show to His disciples that He must go to Jerusalem." There he would, "Suffer many things from the elders and chief priests and scribes, and be killed, and be raised the third day. Then Peter took Him aside and began to rebuke Him, saying, 'Far be it from You, Lord; this shall not happen to You!' But He turned and said to Peter, 'Get behind me Satan! You are an offense to Me, for you are not mindful of the things of God, but the things of men.' Then Jesus said to His disciples, 'If anyone desires to come after Me, let him deny himself, and take up his cross, and follow Me. For whoever desires to save his life will lose it, but whoever loses his life for My sake will find it. For what profit is it to a man if he gains the whole world, and loses his own soul? For the Son of Man will come in the glory of His Father with His angels, and then He will reward each according to His works. Assuredly, I say to you, there are some standing here who shall not taste death till they see the Son of Man coming in His kingdom'" (Matthew 16:16+21-28).

It is possible, through Peter's example to grasp the revelation, "Jesus is the Christ, the Son of the living God," but not grasp His cross for our daily lives. This is being mindful of the things of men, not the things of God. The reason is because the disciples were attached to the idea of ruling and reigning with Christ, but not to the realization of following Christ's example of suffering the cross. This conscience of being mindful of the things of men, no matter how piously camouflaged, will endanger carnal Christians of allying themselves with Satan and become an offense to Jesus Christ. The only way we can be mindful of the things of God is to daily take up our cross and follow Jesus.

It is possible standing there, mindful of the things of men, to gain the whole world and lose one's soul. But standing here, mindful of the things of God, it is possible to never taste death, but instead see the glorious appearing of our Lord Jesus Christ. One mindset melts as a snowman in the heat of Mystery Babylon and attempts to gain the things of men by receiving the Anti-Christ's mark. The other mindset stands firm, mindful of the things of God by rejecting the Anti-Christ's mark. They marvel with the shepherds over the birth, death and resurrection of our savior until he returns as "King of Kings and Lord of Lords!" It is my hope, you will be inspired to renew your commitment to the Lordship of Jesus Christ. And begin to honor the weekly attendance of the house of the Lord, so God can impart the faith and patience you will need in these latter days. That you will begin to pick up your Bible and read it once again, spending quiet times with the Lord and allowing His presence to fill your meditations with the assurance of salvation.

When the mark of the Anti-Christ is implemented, every Christian is going to need the faith and patience of God. The scriptures declare, "That every man should eat and drink and enjoy the good of all his labor-it is a gift of God" (Ecclesiastes 3:13). It is God who blessed man with all of these pleasures. However, Satan who is the thief has come to "steal, kill and destroy" (John 10:10). During the Anti-Christ's reign, Satan seeks to control these pleasures and offer them in exchange for allegiance to the Anti-

Christ by subjecting man to the microchip-mark. During this time, Satan will be tempting Christians just as he tempted Jesus in the wilderness. Satan said, "If You will worship before me, all will be Yours." Our reply will be the same as Christ, "Get behind Me, Satan! For it is written, You shall worship the Lord your God, and Him only you shall serve" (Luke 4:7-8).

Consider the illumination you possess in your soul as a Christian. "You are the Christ, the Son of the living God!" Jesus said, "Flesh and blood has not revealed this to you, but My Father who is in heaven." God alone has given you the key to His kingdom of heaven, which the gates of hell can not prevail against (Matthew 16:16-19). Guard this treasure with all of your heart, soul, mind and body, for only God can give you this revelation, which grants you the key to overcoming Mystery Babylon with all of its Satanic fury. Moreover, when Jesus appears on the "day of the Lord" you will rule and reign with Christ in His kingdom, because you will have overcome!

Appendix A

Fifty Plus Scripture Clues Profiling the Anti-Christ

Revelation

1. Comes out of the seven heads and ten horns. 13:1
2. The mortal wound is healed & the world follows. 13:3
3. He is authoritatively successful; "who can make war with him!" 13:4
4. He is blasphemous toward all that is God. 13:1+5-6 // (16:13)
5. He over comes the saints. 13:7
6. Honor is given to him by the pagan world. 13:11-12
7. The dragon that speaks like a beast honors him. (13:11-12)
8. The dragon causes all to worship him. 13:11-12
9. He performs signs, like fire falling from heaven in the sight of men. 13:13
10. He deceives people. 13:14
11. He makes an image to be worshipped. 13:14
12. He causes the image to come alive and speak audibly. 13:15
13. He imposes a death penalty to those who refuse to worship the image. 13:15
14. He forces all to take a mark in order to buy and sell. (13:16-17)
15. The number of the beast is 666. 13:18
16. He is from the bottomless pit. 17:7-8
17. He is the eight King in a progression of seven previous kings. 17:11
18. He administrates a coalition of the kingdoms of the world. 17:12-13
19. The Lamb overcomes him. 17:14

20. He gathers the world against Christ at Armageddon. (19:19)

21. He is captured along with the false prophet and cast into the lake of fire. 19:20

22. The dragon is cast into the bottomless pit. 20:1-3

23. The dragon is release after a thousand years to deceive for a short season. 20:7-9

24. The dragon is cast into the lake of fire. 20:10

Daniel

25. Seek to slay many that do not have understanding. (2:12-13+28)

26. His image is gold, and his kingdom is a mixture of clay and iron. 2:31

27. God gives his authority to rule. 2:37

28. He rules over the whole earth. 2:38 // 4:22 Rev. (13:7)

29. He makes an image to be worshipped. 3:1

30. The image is connected to 666, as in 60 cubits, 6 cubits and 6 instruments. 3:1+5

31. All nations and cultures are commanded to worship him. 3:4-5 Rev. 13:12

32. He gathers all governing authorities to worship. 3:2-3 (Rev. 17:13+17)

33. Non-cooperation is penalized with death. 3:6 Rev. (13:5)

34. One besides himself commands the people to worship the image. 3: 4 Rev. 13:11-12

35. The Anti-Christ's Babylonians (Chaldeans) accuse the saints over worship. 3: 8 Revelation 12:10+17 // 16:6 (17:6 // 18:24 // 19:2 // 20:4)

36. His government flourishes. 4:4 Rev.13: 4

37. He is a man who has the heart of a beast. 4:16 (Rev.14: 9)

38. Seven years are connected to his beastly rule. 4:16 (Rev.13: 5 + 12:14)

39. His kingdom is given to another. 4:17 Rev.11: 15

40. He is judged for his behavior. 4:31 Rev.19: 19-20

41. He worships gods of gold and silver. 5:4 Rev. (chp.18)

42. He has something written against him. 5:5

43. His judgement comes quickly. 5:30 Rev. 18:10-11 (Rev.19: 20)

44. He makes war with the saints. 7:21 Rev.13: 7

45. He speaks great words against God. 7:25 Rev. (13:5-6)

46. He comes in the context of peace. 11:21+24 (1Thess.5: 3)

47. He works deceptively. 11:23 Rev. 13:14

48. He distributes the saint's wealth.11:14+24+28+33+39 // 12:7 Heb.10:34 Mt. 24:43

49. He has intelligence with those who forsake the holy covenant. 11:30 Mt.24: 10

50. He magnifies himself as God. 11:36 2 Thess.2: 4

51. He desolates the temple. 8:13 2 Thess. 2:4

52. He comes with lying signs and wonders 9:24-25 2 (Thess.2:9 Rev. 13:13-14)

53. He regards the God of forces. 11:38

54. He does not regard the god of his fathers. 11:37

55. He does not desire women. 11:37

56. He sets up his palace in Israel. 11:45

Appendix B   What Money Can and Can Not Buy!

Money will buy:
A bed but not sleep.
A steak but not an appetite.
Books but not wisdom.
Finery but not a sunset.
A house but not a home.
Luxuries but not peace.
Amusement but not joy.
A crucifix but not salvation.
A church pew but not heaven.

210

Appendix C   **Titles of the "day of the Lord"**

Old Testament

The "day of the Lord"
Isaiah 2:12 // 13:6+9 // 46:10
Ezekial 13:5
Joel 1:15 // 2:1 // 2:11 +31 // 3:14
Amos 5:18 +20
Obadiah 15
Zephaniah 1:7+14
Zechariah 14:1
Malachi 4:5

"The day of the wrath of the Lord" Ezekial 7:19
"The day of the Lord's wrath" Zephaniah 1:18
"The day of His fierce anger" Isaiah 13:13
"The day of doom" Jeremiah 51:2
"The day of the Lord's anger" Lamentations 2:22
Zephaniah 2:2-3
"The day of the Lord's vengeance" Isaiah 34:8 // 61:2 //
63:4
"The day of punishment" Isaiah 10:3

New Testament

"The day of judgment" Matthew 10:15 // 11:24 Mark
6:11
"The last day" John 6:39-40+44+54 // 11:24 // 12:48
"The day of the Lord" Acts 2:20   1 Thessalonians 5:2
2 Peter 3:10
"The day of wrath" Romans 2:5
"The day of our Lord Jesus Christ" 1 Corinthians 1:8

"The day of the Lord Jesus" 1 Corinthians 5:5
2 Corinthians 1:14
"The day of Jesus Christ" Philippians 1:6
"The day of Christ" Philippians 1:10 // 2:16
2 Thessalonians 2:2
"That day" 1 Thessalonians 5:4 2 Thessalonians 1:10
// 2:3 2 Timothy 1:12+18 // 4:8
"The day" Hebrews 10:25
"The day of visitation" 1 Peter 2:12
"The day of judgment" 2 Peter 2:9 // 3:7 1 John 4:17
"The day of God" 2 Peter 3:12
"Judgment of the great day" Jude 6
"Great day of His wrath" Revelation 6:17
"Great day of God almighty" Revelation 16:14

Appendix: D   The Seven Seals Opened by the Lamb (Revelation 6)

The seven seals opened by the Lamb are not plagues, but symbols or pictures of what is happening on the face of the earth. The first four seals are pictures of different colored horses that represent according to the Prophet Zechariah, the "four spirits of heaven, who go out from their station before the Lord of all the earth." (Zechariah 6:2-5) Each seal pertaining to the four horses are introduced with the refrain, "Come and See." The phrase is used by Jesus in the New Testament to invite disciples to participate in relationship with God through His Lordship. The result of that relationship is the ability to come and see, or as Apostle Paul said it, "no one knows the things of God except the Spirit of God." (1 Corinthians 2:11) The last three seals are the consequences or results of the influence of the four spirits.

Seal	Symbol	Author's Comments	Description of Influence or Result
#1	White Horse	Jesus Christ Faithful and true In Righteousness Judges & Makes War (Revelation 19:18)	One with a crown sent to conquer. (The Saints get the victory through following the Lordship and suffering of Jesus Christ)
#2	Red Horse	Satan's Nature To Kill, Steal and Destroy (John 10:10)	He takes peace from the earth and causes people to kill one another.

#3	Black Horse	Mystery Babylon's Economy (Revelation 13&14)	Daily provisions of wheat or barley in exchange for a day's wages. (Denarius = day's wages) But do not harm the oil or wine. (Oil and wine = Spirit's Dominion) Black equals spiritual death if you take the Anti-Christ's mark.
#4	Pale Horse	Spirit of Death Hades Following	Power over a ¼ of the earth, to kill the unrighteous that are destined for hell and eternal punishment.
#5	Saints Under Altar	White Robe The Righteousness Of Christ	The Saints who are martyred for: a. Word of God b. Their Testimony They Cry How long O Lord? They Long for God's vengeance. They are given a white robe, and Told to Rest till brethren join them.
#6	Day of The Lord	Earthquake Sun Moon & Stars	The Unrighteous Cry for the Rocks and the Mountains to fall on them and hide them from the wrath of the Lamb.
#7	Seven Trumpets	Plagues of Wrath Revelation of Christ	Six Trumpets are God's Wrath Seventh Trumpet, the Mystery of God is finished and the kingdoms of this world become the kingdoms of Christ (Revelations 10:7+ 11:15)

Appendix E

The Plagues of Exodus and Paralleled Revelation

Exodus				*Revelation*	
Plagues	**Scripture**	XXXXXXXXXX **Scripture**		**Plagues**	XXXXXXXXXX **Scripture**
1 Rods as serpents	Exodus 7:8-13				
2 Water to blood	Exodus 7:14-25			2nd Trumpet 2nd Bowl 3rd Bowl	Revelation 8:8 Revelation 16:3 Revelation 16:4-6
3 Frogs	Exodus 8:1-15			6th Bowl	Revelation 16:12-14
4 Lice	Exodus 8:16-19				
5 Flies	Exodus 8:20-24				
6 Pestilence	Exodus 9:1-7				
7 Boils	Exodus 9:8-12			1st Bowl	Revelation 16:2
8 Hail	Exodus 9:13-21			1st Trumpet 7th Bowl	Revelation 8:7 Revelation 16:17-21

9 Locust	5th Trumpet	Revelation 9:1-3
10 Darkness	4th Trumpet 5th Trumpet 5th Bowl	Revelation 8:12 Revelation 9:1-3 Revelation 16:10
11 Death of firstborn Exodus 11:4-6 12:29-30		
12 Red Sea parting Exodus 14:21-31		
	7th Trumpet Kingdom of World to Kingdom of Christ	Revelation 11:15
	3rd Trumpet Water is Bitter	Revelation 8:10
	6th Trumpet Great day of His Wrath	Revelation 9:13-21
	6th Bowl 200 Million Army	Revelation 16:12
	4th Bowl Scorching Heat	Revelation 16:8-9

(Exodus references: 9 Locust — Exodus 10:1-15; 10 Darkness — Exodus 10:21-26)

Order Form

Enclose and send check to:

Henry Vandergriff
C/O Lamb Publishing
4519 Laurel Hills Road, Raleigh, NC 27612

Price +**Shipping & Handling**   x **Quantity** =**$Total**

$12.95 each +$2.05 each = $15.00 x _____   = $_____

Mail Book(s) To:

Print Name

_____

Address

_____

City

_____State_____Zip_____

**Send Mystery Babylon Witness Wear Brochure?
Circle Yes/No**

Check out our Web Page: MysteryBabylon.net

Review Of Chapters

One
Jesus Speaks in Babylon
"The Latter Days"

This chapter gives the scriptural basis for ancient Babylon being a picture of Mystery Babylon. It also explains how today's buying and selling and the development of the universal personal identification code is consistent with the Anti-Christ's mark, which precedes the revelation of Jesus Christ's return to the earth. Mystery Babylon's tone is set in this chapter. ....Pg. 13

Two
Revelation's Mystery Babylon
"The New Revealed is the Old Concealed"

Old Testament writings of ancient Babylon are like clues in the puzzle of Mystery Babylon. Ancient Babylon's Nimrod, Nebuchadnezzar and Belshazzar give understanding to Mystery Babylon of Revelation. Through them we learn that Mystery Babylon is a spirit and not a geographical location. ....Pg. 27

Three
Mystery Babylon is Alive and Well!
"The Covetous Spirit"

If Mystery Babylon's spirit is alive today, what, when, where and how is it revealed in our presence society? A brief review of present world events reveals its pervasive influence. A sudden enlightenment comes to the reader at this point, as he realizes we are already entrapped in Mystery Babylon. ....Pg. 37

The Author

Henry Vandergriff was born in 1953 and raised in Roanoke, Virginia. He experienced salvation in September of 1971. Upon graduation from college, he helped found Cornerstone church in his hometown where he served as a deacon, an elder and eventually became a staff member as the Assistant Pastor and Business Manager. Since 1983, Henry has been the founding Pastor of Lamb's Christian Center, located near the Research Triangle Park of Raleigh, North Carolina. He is extremely well traveled, having visited twenty countries on four continents. Henry graduated from the University of Virginia Polytechnic Institute with a Bachelor of Science in Business and a Major in Marketing. Prior to the ministry, he served as an executive account representative. He has run a successful contracting business since 1985 and has been married since 1977 to his lovely wife Linda, with whom he has six children.